WIN-WIN
INFLUENCE

WIN-WIN
INFLUENCE

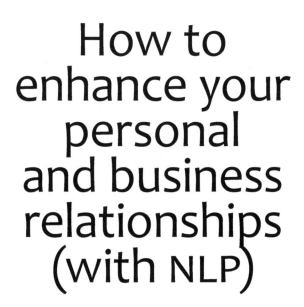

How to
enhance your
personal
and business
relationships
(with NLP)

ROGER ELLERTON, PHD, CMC

The information in this book is not intended as a substitute for business, family, psychological or other counseling, consulting or coaching. The purpose of this book is to educate and entertain. The author and publisher disclaim any responsibility or liability resulting from actions advocated or discussed in this book.

Library and Archives Canada Cataloging in Publication

Ellerton, Roger R. W.
Win-win influence : how to enhance your personal and business
relationships (with NLP) / by Roger Ellerton.

Includes index.
Also issued in electronic format.
ISBN 978-0-9784452-4-9

1. Neurolinguistic programming. 2. Influence (Psychology).
3. Interpersonal communication. 4. Business communication.
I. Title.

BF637.N46E45 2012   158'.9   C2012-903752-4

Editing by Patricia Fry, www.patriciafry.com
Book design by Fiona Raven, www.fionaraven.com
Printed in the USA

Published by:
Renewal Technologies Inc.
688 Spithead Road,
Howe Island, Gananoque, Ontario
Canada K7G 2V6

www.renewal.ca

Acknowledgments

MANY PEOPLE PLAY a role in the final form and success of a book. Over the years, I have met thousands of people. Each of these individuals has in some way affected my thinking about myself, others and the way that I interact with people. My sincere thanks to all of these people as they have influenced my thoughts and what I chose to include in this book.

I am grateful to those who introduced me to neuro-linguistic programming (NLP) and related methodologies. I also want to acknowledge all of the students who attended my NLP training classes. Through your questions and willingness to explore what is possible, you enhanced my understanding of influence and thus made this book just that much better.

More specifically, I wish to extend my deepest gratitude to Sandy Peart Freeman who encouraged me to continue my work on this book when my focus was lacking and who made many substantial suggestions to an earlier draft.

I am also very appreciative of Jessica Byrne and Gary Cameron who reviewed an earlier draft and made many valuable suggestions and comments.

Patricia Fry, as editor, fixed my grammatical errors and identified or re-wrote paragraphs that needed improved clarity and, I trust, added to your reading enjoyment.

Fiona Raven once again worked her magic in designing the interior layout and a cover that reflects the spirit of this book, and on which I am proud to have my name.

Finally, I would like to thank my friends and family members, especially my mother, Irene, my children, Kim, Deanna, Nick, and Matt who, by just being themselves, gave me critical feedback on my influence skills or lack thereof and reasons for getting much better.

Contents

Preface

Developing and perfecting influence skills is a continuous work in progress. If followed and practiced, the ideas, tips and processes described in this book will assist you in improving your influence results with anyone you come in contact with in a manner that achieves a win-win, mutually acceptable result. The emphasis is on expanding your influence skills and results in everyday situations—family discussions, boss-employee interactions and informal conversations. If you are directly or indirectly involved in sales, marketing or negotiation, you will find that the concepts described in this book will enhance your results in these areas, as well. While I often discuss only one of these situations (business or personal relationships, for example), related to a particular topic, be aware that the material is applicable in virtually all influence situations, including your own.

Are you as successful in influencing others as you could be? If asked to sell something—especially your own skills and abilities—do you freeze in your tracks or figuratively run screaming from the room? Or when negotiating a purchase or course of action, do you cave in at the first opportunity and, once again, sacrifice your needs for someone else's? Maybe you hold back from influencing family members, friends or coworkers, simply because you want to avoid a potential confrontation or because you do not know how to connect with the other person.

Whether you realize it or not, you are constantly influencing other people's thoughts about you and your ideas and about themselves and the actions they can take. You do this through your actions as well as your inactions.

This book is based on the concept of influencing others to achieve what you desire, while helping them achieve their needs as well—a win-win approach. Whenever you engage another person—through email or a telephone call, by sending flowers, in person, during a public presentation or in an internet blog—it is an influence opportunity gained or lost depending on what you do and say.

Win-win influence is about respectful communication where both parties feel valued, safe and willing to enter into a mutually beneficial agreement. One of the best, if not *the* best, communication models is neuro-linguistic programming (NLP), which forms a fundamental part of this book. As with any powerful tool, it can be misused. Indeed, it is possible to find NLP/hypnosis books that emphasize hypnotic and slick language patterns to take advantage of others. For me, this is not win-win, although some of those authors will attempt to convince you that the end justifies the means.

If you are looking for tips and techniques to persuade others to your way of thinking or to buy your idea, product or service without regard for their needs or aspirations, then please look elsewhere. This is not about trying to make someone feel good about buying your offering when it does not suit their needs. On the other hand, if you want ideas, tips and an effective process to engage family, friends, coworkers, business associates or customers in a conversation that has the potential for both of you to achieve your goals and open doors to future interactions, then this book is for you.

My intention in writing this book is to provide you with a usable process for improving your influence abilities, your results and your enjoyment in participating in influence situations, including sales and negotiations. Join me in an exploration designed to put into practice useful and effective ideas for improving your influence abilities.

Roger Ellerton
Howe Island, Ontario, Canada

1.

Introduction

1.1. OVERVIEW

Influence—What Is It?

Everyone lives by selling something.

—*Robert Louis Stevenson*

Whether you are a parent, son/daughter, friend, employee, manager or salesperson, you are constantly influencing others to accept you, your ideas, products or services[1]. Those who masterfully present themselves and their ideas in a win-win manner, get ahead. Those who do not, may reap short-term gains and eventually fail in their objective.

Simply having a chat over coffee with a new friend is an influence opportunity that provides both of you with the chance to assess if there is an opening for future interactions. Many of us are fearful of influence opportunities. Perhaps this is because we do not want others to see us as overly demanding, interfering or needy or we worry about being led astray by salespeople, family members or well-intentioned friends. As a result, we often shy away from fully presenting our needs or fully exploring the needs of others.

This book is designed to teach you how to present your needs and have them satisfied while helping others get their needs met. In most cases, this requires compromise. However, it is compromise without giving away what is important to you or pushing others into unnecessary corners. In some cases, it means that

---

1 To avoid overuse of the words "idea, product or service", they will often be referred to as "idea" or "offering."

both parties will agree to disagree. If done in a respectful manner, it encourages future discussions with the potential of reaching a mutually satisfactory agreement on the current matter or some other subject.

Influence is a process—a series of steps with flexibility at each step to take into account the current context and needs of everyone involved. Chapters 3 through 7 document this flow and the actions that are appropriate at each step.

Often people associate manipulation with influence. And you can easily argue that influence includes manipulation. In this book, we focus on win-win influence, which is at the other end of the influence spectrum. For me, win-win influence can be summed up as: Is what you are doing reasonable, ethical, legal, moral and in alignment with the other person's needs, as you understand his[2] needs and given you have taken time to determine them? If all of these conditions are satisfied, then your interaction is win-win.

How important is the ability to influence others? No matter whether you are a businessperson, teacher, parent, stay-at-home spouse, employee or manager, dealing with people is probably the most important activity you undertake throughout the course of your day. A number of years ago, research sponsored by the Carnegie Foundation for the Advancement of Teaching and later confirmed at the Carnegie Institute of Technology discovered that even in engineering, about 15 percent of one's financial success is due to one's technical knowledge and about 85 percent is due to interpersonal skills *(How to Win Friends & Influence People*, Dale Carnegie, p. xiv, revised 1981).

What is NLP?

NLP—built on solid theoretical underpinnings from anthropology, neurology, psychology, physiology, linguistics (transformational grammar), systems theory, general semantics, cybernetics and communication theory—is one of the best models for understanding how humans communicate and make sense of the world around them. When you understand this model and master the basic concepts, you have significantly improved your chances of positively influencing yourself and others.

Neuro refers how you take in information—your sense organs: visual (see), auditory (hear), kinesthetic (tactile touch or emotional feeling), gustatory (taste) and olfactory (smell). *Linguistic* refers to how, in your mind, you put language to

---

2 To avoid the use of "he/she" or excessive alternating between "he" and "she", I will refer to the other person as "he".

what you have experienced or expect to experience—pictures, sounds, feelings, tastes, smells and words. *Programming* refers to your habits, patterns, programs, rituals and strategies—those things you do without really thinking about them.

How to Get the Most Value from This Book

Each chapter begins with an introduction to and an overview of the chapter. Collectively, the overviews offer a summary that can be used as a quick introduction to the material or a review after having read the book. Read the rest of the book, together with the overview sections, for a thorough approach to improving your communication and influence skills.

To master the material in this book and to make a significant improvement in your influence capabilities I suggest the following process:

- Have an outcome—what do you plan to achieve from reading this book?
- Take your time to fully read each chapter and explore how you can put the information to work for you.
- Use the information and material presented.
- Be flexible and open to new ideas.
- Teach someone else what you are learning.
- Adjust and become comfortable using the information in a way that best suits you and meets your needs.
- Make win-win influence a way of life.

1.2. INFLUENCE—WHAT IS IT?

Influence may be the highest level of human skills.

—*Author Unknown*

According to the *Merriam-Webster Dictionary* (www.merriam-webster.com, December 2011), influence is "the power or capacity of causing an effect in indirect or intangible ways." We all strive to have influence in some way, be it over ourselves, our loved ones, colleagues or clients in terms of their actions, thoughts or beliefs. This may be achieved through physical strength, financial clout, positions we hold, respect or the strength of our argument. The most rewarding and long-lasting influence is based on all involved parties being respected and having their needs and aspirations recognized and acknowledged and satisfied to the fullest degree possible. As a result, those involved will welcome similar future interactions.

Be it at home, work, with friends or strangers, you consciously or unconsciously influence others on a daily basis—through your choice of words, tone of voice and body language—to accept your ideas or to accept you. Indeed, any communication with others or yourself has an intended outcome that can be viewed as an attempt to influence. Influence is ever-present, whether you are conscious of it or not and regardless of the intent or name applied to it.

Sometimes you achieve what you want by accident. Other times you achieve nothing through your efforts or the exact opposite of what you hoped for. Influence—positive or negative—can even occur when you are not present, as action or lack of action can speak louder than words. For example, if your spouse expects you home and you are late without letting him know what is happening, then you have created a negative influence situation by not being aware of and addressing his needs. On the other hand, if you are away from home, yet leave a tender note of explanation and maybe a special gift that your spouse will easily find, you have created a positive influence situation.

Those who are successful influencers achieve their personal objectives while respecting the needs and aspiration of others, and thus preserving and cultivating these relationships for future mutually beneficial interactions. Yet, how many people achieve their needs by consciously or unconsciously ignoring or discounting the needs of others, potentially damaging the opportunity for future meaningful collaborations? Then there are still others who go out of their way to avoid being seen to influence others or avoid significant influence opportunities and thus diminish the potential of achieving their own dreams and desires.

Each of us has a preferred way for being influenced, and we tend to (consciously or unconsciously) influence or motivate other people in the way that we prefer to be influenced. However, the other person[3] may have very different needs and different strategies for "buying" or being influenced. Win-win influence involves understanding the true needs and desires of the other person, understanding his criteria for action, and finally presenting your offering in a way that is congruent with his known needs and values. An influence opportunity, when done appropriately, should leave no one the loser. Everyone should feel as if their needs were met and the right decisions were made.

Influence as a Process

Some people see influence as a single activity—present your idea and argue for it until the other person agrees. Actually, influence is a process—a series of steps,

---

3 The term "other person" occurs quite frequently. This other person may in your situation be a child, parent, spouse, coworker, friend, client or boss. To provide some variety, from time to time, I will use "colleague" or "client" to represent this person and allow you to add in your own mind any special significance with regard to this person.

with flexibility at each step to take into account the current context and needs of everyone involved. People have different needs, interests and habits/rituals for accepting or rejecting your idea. As well, different contexts can have a major impact on how the influence process unfolds. This is why you should never assume that the way you previously influenced a friend will work the next time you see him. What you learned from the previous experience is a good start, but you also need to notice if his needs, situation or outside influences have changed.

Influence is critical in leadership, negotiation, teamwork, gaining co-operation and getting others to buy into your ideas. Understanding the influence process will assist you in achieving your goals at work and at home in an effective and ethical manner. The process works equally well whether you are the seller or buyer of the idea.

The details and exact steps may differ depending on the context, however the basic steps in the influence process are:

- Know your needs (RIGHTS[4]) and the benefits of your offering.
  o Know your desired outcome.
  o Have a backup plan.
  o Promote the benefits.
- Prepare in advance.
  o Obtain as much information as you can about the other person—his RIGHTS and how he experiences the world e.g. visual, auditory or does he strive to achieve or to fix problems. These and many other ideas are covered in later chapters.
- Create a space of trust and safety.
- Gain an understanding of the other person.
  o Verify your previous information about this person and ask questions.
- Bridge the gap. There will be a gap between your respective needs until you have an agreement.
  o Acknowledge current positions.
  o Present information and ask questions to raise doubts in the other person's mind about his current position or in your mind as to whether your offering will best meet his needs or does it need modification.
  o Explore alternatives.
  o Confirm agreement.

---

4 RIGHTS are discussed in detail in section 3.2 "Know Your RIGHTS".

Manipulation or Win-Win Influence?

All communication has an influence component to it—e.g. making a telephone call to a loved one just because you want to. The difference between manipulation and win-win influence is the *intention* behind the communication. Some people, when they think of influence, recall memories of being manipulated to agree or do something against their better judgment. In fact, you could argue that influence covers a large range from manipulation (influencing others to do what you want them to do without taking into account their needs) to a win-win approach[5].

To avoid being manipulated, set your own outcomes with clear boundaries. As long as the final agreement is within your conditions, you have not been manipulated. If, on the other hand, the final agreement is outside your boundaries, then the possibility exists that you have been or allowed yourself to be manipulated. If, during an influence situation, you are presented with new information and, on your own, you choose to modify your boundaries and the agreement is within these new boundaries, then, unless the presenter has knowingly given incorrect information, this is not manipulation.

Manipulation doesn't work in the long run because when you've been manipulated, important values have been violated. Manipulation includes behaviors such as bullying, coercion, lying and harassment. And who wants a relationship that isn't built on safety and trust?

Are you inadvertently manipulating others? Is what you are doing reasonable, ethical, legal, moral and in alignment with the other person's needs—as you understand his needs, given you have taken time to determine them? If all of these conditions are satisfied, then your interaction is win-win.

> The most important persuasion tool you
> have in your entire arsenal is integrity.
>
> —*Zig Zigler*

1.3. WHAT IS NLP?

Neuro-Linguistic Programming

NLP is one of the best models for understanding how humans communicate and make sense of the world around them. When you understand this model

---

5 Both parties assist each other to satisfy their respective needs. If this is not possible, they agree to disagree without animosity or hard feelings. Also included is influencing others to do what they want to do (have declared in some fashion) but might not yet be doing.

and master the basic concepts, you have significantly improved your chances of positively influencing yourself and others.

Neuro refers to your neurology—your sense organs: visual (see), auditory (hear), kinesthetic (tactile touch or emotional feeling), gustatory (taste) and olfactory (smell). You experience or perceive events/information via these means.

Linguistic refers to how you use the language of the mind—pictures, sounds, feelings, tastes, smells and words, referred to as internal representations—to remember, represent and make sense of a particular experience or to forecast a future experience. For example, recall the last time you had a loving conversation with a family member. When you remember this event, can you see a picture in your mind or can you hear sounds (perhaps your family member spoke in a particular tone of voice or there were sounds in the background)? What about tastes and smells? And how were you feeling?—happy, excited? Add in specific words that represent some form of code (e.g. relationship, love), and this is how you remember or put language to an event or experience.

Think about the next time you engage a family member or friend in an influence situation. What pictures, sounds, feelings, tastes and smells (if relevant) come to mind? Do you envision yourself being successful? Or failing? Or is the image nondescript? The pictures, sounds, feelings, tastes, smells and words that you use to describe your future experiences have a bearing on what actually happens. You do create your own reality!

Programming refers to your habits, patterns, programs, rituals and strategies—those things you do without really thinking about them. If it is a workday, do you follow a particular routine as you get ready? Perhaps you like to lie in bed an extra five minutes after the alarm goes off. Do you put on the coffee right away or have a shower first? If you take time to look at what you do, you will see a pattern that you follow in getting ready for work. If, for some reason you don't follow that pattern, do you find yourself feeling that something is missing?

Having a ritual for getting up in the morning or any other regularly performed activity is useful. You do not have to take time each day to rediscover it. For the most part, you run it at an unconscious level, giving your conscious mind time and resources to handle other things (for example, *How am I going to make a difference in the meeting with my boss today?*).

Similarly, each of us has a ritual, habit or tactic for buying into an idea or product. When presenting an idea, the more you can match your approach with the programming of the other person, the more comfortable he will feel and the more open he will be to what you are promoting.

Mindlessly, or even consciously, following a habit or program can have unwanted consequences, as well. Particularly if it is a habit or program that worked well to keep you safe or get you what you wanted when you were five years old. Are you are still running this program as an adult? Think about how you engage a certain family member or coworker. Do you have a way of engaging him to avoid a confrontation? Or if you want a confrontation, do you engage him differently?

To further illustrate these unconscious programs, many of us are fully functioning, capable, decisive adults, until we cross the threshold of our parents' home. Then we revert to those old patterns or habits that we exhibited as a child. We may manifest similar behaviors when engaging in a business meeting or sales opportunity in which we perceive the other person as powerful, an expert or the situation as unsafe. Do your behaviors change if the other person is a subordinate or perceived to be weak?

NLP's Origin

NLP has its origin in the early 1970s when a young college student (Richard Bandler) and an associate professor (John Grinder, PhD [transformational grammar]) at the University of California in Santa Cruz studied the work of Fritz Perls (gestalt therapy), Virginia Satir (family systems therapy) and Milton Erickson (hypnotherapy). They integrated their findings with results from transformational grammar (Noam Chomsky), cognitive psychology (George A. Miller, Eugene Galanter, and Karl H. Pribram) and anthropology and systems theory (Gregory Bateson). Their intention was to explore how experts achieved the results that they did. In describing these processes they were able to create a model that could be taught to and used by others to generate similar results. Thus, NLP is a model that is built on solid theoretical underpinnings from anthropology, neurology, psychology, physiology, linguistics (transformational grammar), systems theory, general semantics, cybernetics and communication theory.

NLP is more than just techniques. It is a curiosity about how people who are high achievers (in any field) accomplish what they actually set out to do. It is also a methodology that assists you in discovering those thinking and communication patterns that prevent you from being successful and shows you how to achieve the results of successful people. That is, NLP is a process for discovering experts' patterns of excellence, and making these effective ways of thinking and communicating available for personal benefit or to assist others.

So what is NLP? Some NLP experts claim it is a form of therapy, as it began with the modeling of therapists Perls, Satir and Erickson. Indeed, most of the original NLP books were written from a therapy point of view and NLP can claim countless significant successes in this area. You can also argue that NLP is more about psychological health (self-actualization) rather than therapy, as Perls, Satir and Bateson were part of the Human Potential Movement that is based on Maslow's idea of modeling the best and healthiest in human nature.

Some NLP proponents confuse NLP with hypnosis or hypnotherapy, as many of the basic NLP principles and techniques are a result of understanding how Milton Erickson approached his work. The basis of Erickson's success was his sensory acuity (paying attention), his ability to read nonverbal behavior, his ability to establish rapport with his clients, his skill with language patterns and his beliefs about his clients e.g.:

- Every behavior has a positive intention.
- There are no resistant clients, only inflexible therapists.

And then there are those who would argue that, since Perls, Satir and Erickson were also world-class communicators, NLP is more about communication—how people use words to inform themselves and others, and, in so doing, create an interpretation of reality, which then has a bearing on the behaviors they manifest. The NLP communication model provides us with a very useful tool for understanding communication issues (with ourselves, others and work teams) and how these issues can be addressed. The processes used by Perls, Satir and Erickson were discovered by careful observation or modeling. Thus, we are directed to the process of modeling—modeling excellence in whatever form it may be (e.g. sales, public speaking, managing, parenting)—and then showing others how they can use this information so they, too, may achieve similar results.

According to Michael Hall (www.neurosemantics.com), a noted NLP researcher and trainer, "And if they had really focused on that (communication), they might have turned to focus on business and if they had done that, the field of NLP could have possibly discovered the field of coaching and would today own it. But they didn't. It would be many years later before NLP applications for business would develop." NLP has had a significant impact on business. After all, business runs on its ability to communicate within its organization and with external partners, customers and the general population. Now, many more NLP books are being written from a communication, business or coaching perspective.

NLP had its origins in modeling outstanding therapists, and today experts in virtually all fields have been modeled for their excellence. The resulting models have found application in all areas of human endeavor—education, health, sports, management, and, perhaps most importantly, interpersonal relations. Indeed, it would be difficult to attend any workshop or training course involving human interaction—sales, alternative dispute resolution, negotiation, presentation skills, communication, management—that did not contain NLP concepts, although these concepts are often not identified as originating from NLP.

1.4. WHO WILL BENEFIT FROM THIS BOOK?

A variety of audiences will find the information in this book useful:

- Managers who wish to connect with their staff in a respectful and practical manner. Indeed, it can be said that an organization is only as strong as the relationships between its people.
- Coworkers who want to leave derision and conflict behind in order to create a workplace worthy of their talents.
- Human resource recruiters who can represent their company in terms of candidate needs, especially when qualified applicants are in short supply.
- Job applicants who want to get a leg up on their competition.
- Family members who are looking for effective ways to create long-term, warm, supporting bonds with other family members.
- Teachers who wish to connect with their students in a different way and truly make a difference.
- Coaches and those in the helping professions who are looking for effective ways to support their clients.
- Consultants who wish to prepare consulting reports for senior management in a way that senior management can buy into them and that the value of their expertise is not lost.
- Sales staff who are looking to expand their skill set to generate profitable referrals and long-term clients.
- Presenters who wish to influence their audiences.
- Website designers and bloggers, who want to present their ideas services and products in a way that resonates for potential clients.
- People responding by e-mail, so the recipient is open to fully considering their thoughts.

1.5. HOW TO GET THE MOST VALUE FROM THIS BOOK

This book can be viewed as two books in one.

- The short version. Each chapter begins with an "Overview." Collectively, the overviews provide you with an overall summary that can be used as a quick introduction to the material or a review after having read the book. The overviews will also allow you to step back, without getting bogged down in too many details, to see that influence is a process and determine where you are in that process.

- The detailed version. The rest of each chapter builds on the overview, providing a detailed exploration of that aspect of the influence process with relevant real world examples.

Due to the non-linear nature of human communication, some information will be relevant to more than one of the steps in the influence process and is covered in detail when first required. To assist you in finding relevant information, references to previously discussed material are included as is a comprehensive index.

To master the material in this book and to make a significant improvement in your influence capabilities, I suggest the following process:

- **Have an outcome**. The law of attraction tells us to focus on what we want in life. What do you want for yourself? Take a few moments to write down at least one outcome to focus on as you read this book.
- **Take time to fully read each chapter**. When you come across a new idea, ask yourself: "How can I use this? Can this be modified to make it more useful in my situation?" If, on the first reading, an idea or concept does not seem appropriate, challenge it, explore it from many different perspectives to find at least one aspect that has the potential to make a difference in how you interact with others.
- **Use it.** Once you have finished reading a chapter, put the information you have learned into action. There is no failure, only feedback. If, when using the material, things do not work out as planned, ask yourself, "What do I need to learn about myself, others or the world in general so that next time I can do even better?" Do not expect to use all of the information in this book in a particular influence situation. Indeed, during the first couple of opportunities you have, you may only use one or two of the ideas. Notice which ones seem to add the most value for you. Practice using them. Then gradually add other ideas as you work toward being an effective influencer in all areas of your life.
- **Be flexible and open to new ideas.** As you read further in this book, your thoughts about influence, yourself and others may begin to change. Accept that NLP is a very useful model for understanding human dynamics, and that a model is a generalization about some aspect of the world. No model is 100 percent correct. The question is not whether the model is correct; rather, the question is: "Does the model produce useful results?" The answer with regard to NLP is a clear, resounding, "Yes, it does!" As you read this book, you can focus—negatively—on finding the few places where the model may not work or you can accept the general principles and move forward to achieve what is important for you.

- **Teach someone else.** Increase your influence by helping others to improve how they communicate and influence others. If you have difficulty explaining a concept, be open to discussing it with the other person.
- **Make it your own.** The material I have presented here is from what I and others have found useful. You and I are different in a number of ways. Therefore, what I find really useful, you may only find moderately useful and vice versa. So adjust and become comfortable using the information in a way that best suits you and meets your needs.
- **Make win-win influence a way of life.**

The concepts in this book are sound and applicable wherever and whenever you interact with one or more people. If you choose to use and apply them ethically and consistently, they will work. You are limited only by your imagination in your desire to help yourself and others achieve their desires and live the life you choose.

> If you want something you've never had, you must
> be willing to do something you've never done.
>
> —*Thomas Jefferson*

2.

Foundation for Win-Win Influence

2.1. OVERVIEW

Communication skills—your ability to deliver your message in a warm, thoughtful, respectful manner—are often the determining factor in whether you achieve your goals or fall short. The NLP communication model is an effective model for understanding how people communicate and how they influence themselves and others. It explains why people do what they do.

> You can have brilliant ideas, but if you can't get
> them across, your ideas won't get you anywhere.
>
> —*Lee Iacocca*

How Do You Process Information?

At any given moment, you have access to about four billion bits of information that you can see, hear, touch, taste or smell. This is far too much information for anyone to process and so you focus on only that information that you perceive to be important—about two thousand bits of information. That is less than one ten thousandths of a percent of all the information available. If you happen to be a visual person, you will focus more on what you see rather than hear, feel, taste or smell. And it follows that you also create pictures, sounds, feelings tastes and smells in your mind (called internal representations) to remind you of what you have experienced in the past.

If you believe you are not good at something this is the information you will focus on, disregarding many of the times you have succeeded. Unfortunately, based on your observation of a very small part of the information available to you, you will call this interpretation your reality.

Someone else—a family member or coworker, perhaps—will have different beliefs, values and preferences, and will focus on other information. This may overlap with what you have observed or not, depending on the situation. The point is that, based on their observations, they will create what they consider to be reality.

Suppose you are about to engage this person in a conversation to influence him in some way. Perhaps your first thoughts are, *Since I like this idea and I came to this conclusion in the following manner, I will influence him in the same way and he, too, will like it as I do.* However, each of you could have very different interpretations of reality and potentially process and make sense of the world in different ways. If you are to be successful at influencing someone else, you need to understand how he sees the world and what is important to him.

Guiding Principles

NLP has a set of presuppositions or guiding principles that I have found to be very useful in guiding and improving my communication and influence abilities with others. These are not presented as absolute truths, but something to fully consider when engaging others.

- You cannot not communicate.
- Respect the other person's model of the world.
- The person with the most flexibility of behavior will have the most influence.
- There is no failure, only feedback.
- Every behavior has a positive intention.
- The meaning of communication is the response it produces.
- Resistance in another person is a sign of lack of rapport.

Focus on What You Want

Focus your attention and energy on what you want. In the past, you may have focused on what could go wrong—the two thousand bits of information that did not support your desires. Now you have a choice and I encourage you to play the "opposite game." That is, every time you notice (i.e., interpret) something negative about yourself or other people, reassess your interpretation and look for two things you can interpret as positive and supporting of this new view of yourself or them. You will find that your world will begin to change, although it may happen slowly at first. Your positive beliefs about yourself, your coworkers, family and others will strengthen, leading to greater successes.

2.2. HOW YOU PROCESS INFORMATION

The NLP communication model (figure 1) provides interesting and useful insights/into how you process information and how this processing has a bearing on your behaviors and your success in influencing others in a win-win manner:

- You observe an event with your senses (see, hear, feel, taste and smell).
- You generalize, delete and distort (filter) this information according to what you perceive to be important—according to your beliefs, values, decisions, etc.
- You make internal representations (pictures, sounds, feelings, tastes, smells and code words) based on this filtered information, and you call this *reality*.
- These internal representations influence your internal state, which influences your behaviors (external physiology, actions, choice of words and tone of voice).

Changing your filters (beliefs, values, etc.) will affect what you pay attention to and thus how you react to the world around you.

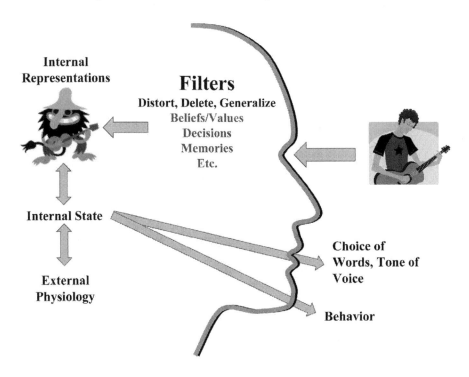

FIGURE 1: NLP COMMUNICATION MODEL

The following sections build on this model and add to your understanding.

Conscious Awareness

At any given moment, your senses and hence your unconscious mind are exposed to about four billion bits of information. Are you consciously aware of all of this information? Of course not. For example, at this moment are you aware of how your left foot feels? I suspect that, until I mentioned it, you were not aware of how your left foot felt. But I'll bet you are aware of it now. Before I drew your attention to your left foot, you didn't perceive the information that was coming to you via your left foot as important—unless you have something wrong with your left foot. Since you did not perceive this information to be important, you filtered it out. What other information are you filtering out at this time? Take a moment to hear what sounds are available to you that you were not fully aware of a few moments ago. Or continue looking at your book, and, without moving your eyes, perhaps you have now become aware of other things you can see.

What's going on here? Of the four billion bits of information available to your unconscious mind, your conscious mind can only process about two thousand bits, or about 0.00005 percent of this information. To consciously process more of this information would either drive you crazy or be such a distraction that you could not function.

What two thousand bits of information does your conscious mind pay attention to? The two thousand bits that it perceives to be important at the time. Before I drew your attention to your left foot, that information was not perceived to be important. Yet, once I mentioned it, it's perceived to be more important.

You've undoubtedly experienced times when you were so completely engaged in reading a book, watching TV or working on a hobby that you were unaware of activities going on around you. Yet, if your newborn cried in a certain way or a family member called for help, you suddenly forgot what you were doing and focused your two thousand bits on these new important needs.

In a conversation or influence situation, you will naturally pay attention to the information that is most important to you, unless you make a concerted effort to also view the situation from your colleague's perspective with a focus on reaching a win-win outcome.

Filters—Deleting, Distorting and Generalizing

What happens to all of this other information? Your brain filters it from your conscious awareness through the following:

- *Deleting* is the process of paying attention to information you perceive to be important and deleting the rest. By eliminating extraneous information, you can attend to what you perceive to be important. In an influence opportunity, you may overly focus on one of your needs at the expense of others. By knowing your and the other person's needs, you have the potential to take a more balanced approach resulting in a better agreement for both parties.

- *Distorting* is the process of changing the relationship between experiences. Distorting can provide you with a different view of reality, which can lead you to seeing and experiencing the world differently from others. This may open up new possibilities for you, and it may lead to disagreements when your interpretation of reality conflicts with that of others. Simplifying, exaggerating and daydreaming are examples of distorting.

- *Generalizing* is the process of taking one or a limited number of experiences and projecting it to other similar experiences. If, for example, as a child you were hurt by your father, you may have generalized this to be wary when engaging your father (and perhaps all men); thus having a major impact on how you approach and what you are able to accomplish in an influence situation that involves men.

What you actually delete, distort and generalize depends on your beliefs, values, language (the meaning you assign to words), decisions and memories you have about the topic at hand, e.g. influence.

If you believe you don't have good influence skills, what two thousand bits of information are you paying attention to? Certainly, it is evidence that will support and thus reinforce this belief. If this reflects your experience, perhaps you should play the opposite game and start paying attention to when you do exhibit good influence skills.

Both types of information are available to you at any given moment. Whichever type you pay attention to reinforces the beliefs/values you already have about yourself or others. What information do you pay attention to (perceive to be important) on a regular basis? Are you creating a world that supports who you can truly be or creating a world that keeps you small?

> If you believe you can or believe
> you can't, you're right.
>
> —*Henry Ford*

An understanding of filters helps to explain why not everyone experiences the world the same way, nor wants the same rewards from life, nor reacts in the same manner to a specific event. This does not make one person right or the other wrong; it's simply that people interpret things differently depending on their filters. And this is critical in an influence situation—the other person most likely does not want what you want, nor are they influenced by the same needs and values as you are.

Internal Representations

Do you remember having breakfast this morning? How do you remember it? Do you see a picture in your mind or are there smells or tastes? Are there sounds—perhaps in your mind you can hear a radio? To remember an event, your mind uses pictures, sounds, feelings, tastes, smells and words. These perceptions of your "outside world" are called *internal representations* and are a function of your filters. Your perceptions are what you consider to be "real," in other words, your reality.

If you and your spouse have breakfast together, your internal representations or perceptions of the occasion will most likely be similar in some ways and different in others, depending on what is important or unimportant to each of you (your filters). Breakfast is not very controversial. However, what about your respective views on how to raise children? Given your different backgrounds, you may, in each of your minds (your internal representations), see, hear and feel differently about how children should behave and hence exhibit significantly different behaviors with your children. Suppose you are about to have a conversation with your spouse on how your children should be raised. Unless each of you is willing to accept that both of you have valid (although different) interpretations of how to raise children based on your beliefs, values and past experiences, and are willing to step outside of your interpretation of reality and be flexible in your approach, you may find the ensuing conversation difficult. In fact, it could result in a major disagreement.

Internal Representations and Behaviors

Would you like to see the effect internal representations have on your behaviors? Then fully play along with me and imagine a dill pickle on a plate in front of you. Notice how it looks. Remember the sound of biting into a crisp, juicy dill pickle as the juice flows across your tongue and all around your mouth. What does that taste like? That's right, take a moment to fully experience the taste of a dill pickle. What I've done is helped you recall certain pictures, sounds, feelings and tastes in your mind. If you've ever eaten a dill pickle, I suspect you are either salivating right now or reacting in some other way to the idea of eating a dill pickle. In either case, I did not ask you to have that physical reaction. You had it in response to the internal representations you made in your mind. This demonstrates that the internal representations you create in your mind influence your physiology. Carrying this further, they influence your choice of words, the tone of voice you use and the behaviors you manifest. In the same way, when you think of a particular family member, friend, customer or coworker, you will create a positive, neutral or negative set of internal representations of him that will influence your body language, choice of words, tone of voice and, in general, how you interact with him. When attempting to influence this person, indeed, all of this will have a major impact on whether or not you reach a win-win agreement.

Now for another exercise: Sit up straight, put a big smile on your face, tilt your head up slightly and breathe deeply. While you do that, attempt to feel sad. I am almost certain that you cannot feel sad without changing your physiology (for example, shallow breathing and rounded shoulders). This illustrates that your physiology influences your state—whether you feel sad or happy—which, in turn, influences your internal representations. Next time you are about to enter an influence situation, you may consider sitting or standing straighter, smiling and breathing deeply in a calm powerful manner to put yourself in a better state of mind.

Consider the following: Through your filters—that is, what you choose to observe—suppose you interpret a coworker's actions to be out of alignment with your beliefs/values. In the blink of an eye, your mind calls up internal representations in the form of pictures, sounds and feelings of previous events that reinforce your assessment of this person (the box you have put him in)—your reality. With these internal representations at the forefront of your mind, what do you think your physiology will be like when you begin to talk to him? What about your tone of voice or the words you use? Given those behaviors, do you think he will fully understand what you are saying and do what you suggest? Most likely not! And what has he done? He's verified your interpretation of reality and proven once more that he is, indeed, the person you made him out to be.

2.3. GUIDING PRINCIPLES

The foundation for NLP is a set of presuppositions (beliefs) about ourselves and the world we live in. These presuppositions also serve as principles to guide how we interact and influence others. I will not claim that these presuppositions are absolutely true in all possible situations. I do believe they are true in the vast majority of situations. You can spend your time trying to find the rare exception to when the presupposition does not hold, or you can acknowledge there may be exceptions and focus on all of the times you can use them to your advantage.

The following presuppositions are very useful for effective communication and enhancing your influence with others. You may find some of them are already part of your life. You may also find one or more of them confusing or unrealistic. In this case, they may be outside of what you currently perceive to be your reality. As a result, there may be value for you to step into this belief and explore what you can discover about yourself and what else is possible.

1. **You cannot not communicate.**
    Often we think we communicate only through the words we say or write. This is not so. You also communicate through your tone of voice, body language and actions. You may say the "right" words, and if your tone of voice or body language is not in alignment with those words, which message is really received? Even no communication sends a message, and it is often not a positive one.

    Have you ever attended a meeting with someone who clearly did not want to be there? Perhaps he was sitting slouched over with arms crossed and little or no expression on this face. How did you feel about being in the same room with him? He certainly influenced the energy within the room, but how much influence did he have for achieving his real needs?

    When interacting with others, be aware of how your mood/thoughts affect your tone of voice, choice of words and body language. Ask yourself, *Is this helpful for achieving my desired outcome*?

    Purchasing a special gift for someone or doing something you know they will like, just because you want to, sends a powerful message. The same is true for not living up to your promises and commitments. Take time to step back and see the impact of your actions on the people around you. Is this really the impression you wish to create or the message you wish to convey?

2. **Respect the other person's model of the world.**
    You have your own unique interpretation of reality—your own view or model of the world—which has a significant unconscious influence on your behaviors. Your interpretation of reality may be quite similar to or differ vastly from another person's.

    We each create our experience of the world differently, because we all have different sets of experiences and filters. You may not understand or agree with my behavior. However, if you had a similar upbringing to mine, you may well have adopted beliefs, values, decisions and interpretations of reality comparable to mine.

    You don't have to agree with the other person's model of the world, only respect that he may see, hear, feel and interpret the world differently than you do. As a result, he may be motivated by different values, make different choices and hence behave differently. It's not personal. He simply has a different perspective of the world.

The other day, I was supporting a friend who is going through some personal difficulties. His chosen course of action is not what I would do and I so wanted to tell him how to do it (my way). But this would not have supported him. Instead, I created a space of trust and safety and asked questions that helped him see other possibilities (reframing, see section 7.4)—possibilities that have much greater potential for success than anything I would have imposed on him.

The Golden Rule states: "Do unto others as you would have others do unto you." Perhaps the Platinum Rule should state: "Do unto others by respecting their model of the world."

3. **The person with the most flexibility of behavior will have the most influence.**

Have you ever been stuck in life, doing the same things repeatedly and each time expecting to get a different result? This is the widely known definition of insanity. If you want your life to be different, doing the same things more often, harder or louder is not the way to change it. You must choose to do something different. If you try one key in a lock and it doesn't fit, would you keep trying the same key repeatedly? Or would you be flexible and try other keys until you find the one that works?

To be effective in an influence situation, you need to be flexible. You know your desired outcome and your best alternative to a negotiated agreement (BATNA see section 3.4). Within this range, you have flexibility to concede on some points and perhaps get more than expected on others. I am sure you have experienced people who are not flexible in their approach. Yes, they may well win that argument. However, in the longer term they have lost much more. Flexibility is not about giving in or throwing in the towel, it is about meaningful, considered compromise that meets a critical need for the other person, while still within your acceptable range of expectations/needs. Effective influence is not about one person winning at the expense of another. It is about each of you reaching an agreement that you both feel good about and having a willingness to participate in future influence situations with each other.

4. **There is no failure, only feedback.**

You do something and it doesn't work out the way you had planned. How often do you interpret this as failure?

Think of young children as they learn to walk. They tentatively stand, maybe attempt a step and fall down. Then, they immediately get up and attempt to walk again. At no time do they view the previous attempt as failure or immediately conclude, *Well, I guess I'm just not a walker!* Instead, they take it as an opportunity to learn and see how far they can get the next time.

How different would it be for you in a conversation or influence situation if, each time something did not work out as planned, you viewed that misstep simply as feedback—an opportunity to learn how not to do something and to become flexible in developing new ways to achieve your intended outcomes? Would this give you permission and encouragement to undertake new things, become more curious and be potentially more successful in life?

> Failure is simply the opportunity to begin
> again, this time more intelligently.
>
> —*Henry Ford*

5. Every behavior has a positive intention.
No matter how strange, hurtful or inappropriate a person's behavior may seem to you, for the person engaging in that behavior, it makes sense in their model of the world. It is predicated upon satisfying a positive intention for them, though not necessarily for you.

For example, assume you are discussing something personal with a family member. Without warning, he bolts from the room. You are confused and a little upset. The key is to appreciate that there is a positive intention behind his behavior. This does not mean that you must view his behavior as positive or acceptable. On the contrary, you may find it quite distasteful. You need to look behind the behavior to discover the positive intention or, if it's not apparent, look for an intention that makes sense in his reality. Knowing his background, explore for a moment what the positive intention could be for him. Is it possible that he felt overwhelmed and needed to get some space so that he could think? Perhaps, in his world, this seemed to be the best possible action he could take. Once you have an understanding of his intention, you can explore alternative ways to help him achieve it and thus render the unwanted behavior unnecessary.

That is, you can accept what happened as feedback, respect his model of the world, explore the possible positive intentions behind his behavior and look at other ways to achieve your outcome while satisfying his positive intention. Be flexible.

Regularly take stock of your own behaviors. Notice the results you are achieving, identify the positive intention behind these behaviors and ask, *Is there a better way to achieve my positive intention?*

6. **The meaning of communication is the response it produces.**

Your intended communication is not always what is understood by the other person. It does not matter what your intention is; what matters is how the other person interprets your communication and the results you generate from your words, tone of voice, facial expression and body language. People will experience what you say through past successful and unsuccessful family interactions or business dealings. Most of the time, it has nothing to do with you. Quite simply, the way you present your thoughts reminds him of a previous experience and he filters your choice of words and body language through his beliefs, values and memories (pleasant and unpleasant) of previous relationships (personal or business).

During a conversation, you may decide to say something that you consider humorous to lighten up the conversation. However, as the other person processes it through his filters (beliefs, values), he may not find it funny, but the exact opposite. He may have heard something very different from what you intended. You can leave it at that and proceed on with this cloud over your conversation, or you can recognize that your comment did not produce the result you intended. This is the time to be flexible—to find different ways to communicate with him so that you can both carry on this conversation in a meaningful and supportive manner.

7. **Resistance in another person is a sign of lack of rapport.**

Rapport with another person is about trust and safety. If the other person does not trust you or feel safe, either due to your inability to fully explain what is expected of him and the resulting consequences, or because of your tone of voice and body language, he may resist your suggestions. Generally, there are no resistant people, only inflexible communicators.

You can simply read the above presuppositions or you can begin to put them into action and make a difference in how you interact with and influence others. I personally have found them to be very useful in assisting me in improving my communication and influence with others.

2.4. FOCUS ON WHAT YOU WANT

In *The Secret* (Atria Books/Beyond Words, 2006), Rhonda Byrne discusses the law of attraction, which is to focus on what you want in life. The more precisely you focus, the better the law of attraction works. The opposite is also true—the less you focus on what you want, the less you achieve. A significant part of that law, which is often overlooked, is, the more you focus on what you don't want, the more you get of that.

The law of attraction does work and it is not a new discovery. Successful men and women have known, used and been writing about this for some time. James Allen, in his book, *As a Man Thinketh* (1902), said,

> Good thoughts and actions can never produce bad results. Bad thoughts and actions can never produce good results. This is but saying that nothing can come from corn but corn, nothing from nettles but nettles. Men understand this law in the natural world, and work with it. But few understand it in the mental and moral world (though its operation there is just as simple and undeviating), and they, therefore, do not cooperate with it.

3.

Know Your Needs and the Benefits of What You Offer

3.1. OVERVIEW

Critical to your success in any influence situation is knowing what is important to you and how what you offer satisfies what is important to the other person (benefits).

Know Your RIGHTS

Having an understanding of your specific needs and values will provide clarity on what truly is important to you and will help you recognize where you can compromise, suggest trade-offs or hold firm. Although not comprehensive, I have found that specifying your most important needs and values in terms of RIGHTS can stimulate your thought processes and force you to take a more concerted look at your needs and values. RIGHTS is simply an acronym that helps you to identify and remember what is important for you.

To determine your RIGHTS for a particular situation—career, family—think of at least one important need or value for each of the letters. Possible suggestions are:

R — reputation, results, minimize risk.
I — income, information, influence.
G — generosity (philanthropic), goodwill, guarantee.
H — health, happiness, honor.
T — time, timeliness, taste.
S — safety, success, skills.

Know Your Desired Outcome

Your RIGHTS summarize what is important to you in a given context. Your next step is to identify what you will focus on to satisfy these RIGHTS. What is your goal or outcome? Many people formulate their outcome in terms of SMART goals, expressed in terms that are:

- S (specific and simply stated).
- M (measurable and meaningful).
- A (achievable).
- R (realistic and responsible).
- T (timed and focused toward what you want).

Phrasing and assessing your outcome from a SMART perspective has many benefits, however it misses two very important aspects that are covered by MASTERY. Notice that MASTERY includes all of the letters in SMART, plus two others:

- E (ecological—what will be the impact on you, your family or workplace?).
- Y (yearning—are you truly passionate about this outcome?).

Have a Backup Plan

Let's face it, there will be times when your needs and values and those of the other person do not dovetail sufficiently to result in a win-win agreement. You need to recognize these cases and have a "Plan B" that is fully acceptable to you. This Plan B should also follow the MASTERY format, particularly with regard to ecology so that you are not taking this action to spite the other person or for him to feel sorry for you. In negotiation terminology, this Plan B is called a "Best Alternative to a Negotiated Agreement" (BATNA).

Quite simply, if the best agreement you eventually negotiate is better than your BATNA, then you should accept it. Otherwise, consider pursuing your alternative.

Promote the Benefits of Your Offering

Win-win influence is basically, satisfying your RIGHTS while addressing what is important to the other person. Far too often, we promote the features or other interesting pieces of information about our offering, leaving the determination of potential benefits up to the other person. Sometimes this happens because we have not taken time to assess the benefits of our offering. Or we know them in the back of our mind, but are not sure how to present the benefits to the other person. Unfortunately, the other person does not make the connection to a benefit and only focuses on the features, which does not generate a strong desire to buy the product or idea.

To move from features to benefits, use the "So What?" exercise. For each feature, ask yourself "So What?" and explore answers from the other person's point of view. You may need to do this three or four time for each feature until you get something meaningful and motivating for the other person.

If you are in business promoting yourself, a product or service, or are pursuing a career or looking for work, you need to have an elevator speech that will capture the other person's attention and encourage them to want more. This brief introduction (about fifteen seconds or two sentences) conveys the essence of what you, your product or service does. Rather than a descriptive phrase about skills or features, it stresses benefits for the other person.

3.2. KNOW YOUR RIGHTS

If you are not certain on what is important to you, you will not be able to clearly express your needs to others, you may miss an opportunity to influence a critical decision or you may end up agreeing to something that does not truly meet your needs or values. Often, you may feel there's a disconnect between what you are doing and what you want and value. Your actions/desires may be seen as:

- Confusing.
- Unrealistic, given your current resources (finances, education, network) and mindset.
- Lacking passion.

And you may not be fully aware of unforeseen consequences that end up taking you off track.

Having an understanding of your specific needs and values will provide clarity on what truly is important to you and will help you recognize where you can compromise, suggest trade-offs or hold firm. It is also a critical step in formulating your desired outcome in an influence situation. Your needs and values can be tangible, such as possessions, or intangible, such as respect and integrity. Although not comprehensive, I have found that determining your most important needs and values in terms of RIGHTS can stimulate your thought processes and force you to take a more concerted look at your needs and values. It also provides an acronym for remembering what is important to you and, when you're in the middle of an intense conversation, it helps you avoid forgetting about something important. If your specific needs and values do not fully fit the RIGHTS model, that is OK, as it is only a guide. As well, there will be situations where one or more letters in RIGHTS will go lacking and that, too, is OK, provided you have indeed thought fully about your needs and values.

To get in touch with what is important to you, I suggest you find a place absent of distractions. Sit or lie down comfortably and allow your thoughts to go deep inside and explore what is most important to you. As you do, notice which needs and values correspond to the letters in RIGHTS. You may come up with some additional needs or values that do not start with any of these letters. In this case, can you link them to one of these letters so that you have a way of keeping them in mind? It is preferable to express your needs and values in positive terms (toward what you want), e.g. "Safety" rather than "avoid being Hurt." However, there may be occasions to clearly express what is to be avoided or minimized, e.g. "Risk."

To help you identify your RIGHTS, here are some possible suggestions:

R —reputation, results, risk, relationship (connection with others), reduced costs, respect, resourceful, resources, rapport.

I —income, information, influence, image, investment.

G —generosity (philanthropic), goodwill, guarantee, green (environmental concerns), get up and go (energy), grateful, glory, looking good, goals.

H —health, happiness, honor, helpful, heroic, humor, heard.

T —time, timeliness, taste, team, tenure.

S —safety, success, skills, save (money, environment), status, satisfaction.

Bringing this closer to reality, for a family vacation, your needs might be expressed as R (recreation), I (itinerary), G (geographic area), H (healthy), T (time of year), S (safety). On the other hand, if you are in sales, your critical needs might be R (repeat business), I (income), G (gratitude), H (helpful), T (time period [e.g. prior to yearend]), S (success rate).

Some of these suggestions may not appeal to you. However, remember that each of us experiences the world differently. Those that don't resonate for you may be very important to someone else. In the next chapter, we will discuss identifying the RIGHTS of the other person.

What are your most important needs and values—RIGHTS? Are they being met when interacting with others? Knowing your RIGHTS will provide guidance as you engage others—plan for a vacation, involve a family member/coworker in a conversation or make a major purchase. Take a moment now to complete your RIGHTS for career, vacation, relationship, life in general, your next sales opportunity or something that is meaningful to you. You may wish to use the "So What?" exercise described in section 3.5 to gain greater insight.

In the context of _____, my RIGHTS are:

- R

- I

- G

- H

- T

- S

3.3. KNOW YOUR DESIRED OUTCOME

You have a good understanding of your RIGHTS. Now consider, in a given situation, what, specifically, do you want to achieve? E.g. what are your goals? Many people formulate their goals or outcomes as SMART goals. Phrasing and assessing your outcome from a SMART perspective has many benefits, however it misses two very important aspects that are covered by MASTERY. Notice that MASTERY includes all of the letters in SMART, plus two others.

Outcome MASTERY

M   **Measurable**—How will you know if you are making progress and what must happen for you to know you have achieved your desired outcome?

Meaningful—Is your outcome important for you? It needs to be meaningful for you, not someone else.

A   **Achievable**—Do you believe your outcome is achievable? It needs to be achievable in terms of what you believe, not what others believe.

All areas of your life—Are you fully congruent for achieving this outcome or are there conflicts (internal or external) that you need to resolve?

As if now—From this moment on, live as if you already have achieved your outcome. Many famous people have lived their lives as if they had already achieved their dreams long before they became famous. In so doing, they influenced others to think that way about them, as well.

S   **Simple**—Your outcome should describe clearly what you plan to achieve and should be expressed in very simple language and sentence structure. In this way, there is no confusion on what needs to be done.

        Specific—The outcome, "I want more money" is simple, yet not specific. It does not specify when this is to happen or how much more money. The way this desired outcome is currently formed, if someone were to give you one penny, your outcome would be achieved.

T   **Timed**—You must specify an exact time. Saying "tomorrow" or "next month" is not adequate—tomorrow will always be tomorrow.

        Toward what you *do* want—What you focus on is what you get. If your outcome is, "I don't want to fail," your focus is on failing. You will then notice all the signs of potential failure rather than the signs of success. Focusing on what you don't want implies that anything else is acceptable and the outcome you achieve may be worse than what you have now.

        Being aware of what you don't want can be useful to get you moving. To sustain this movement, you need to have something you're moving toward.

E   **Ecological**—Is your outcome in alignment with your values? What is the potential impact now and in the future on your family or work and your health and well-being?

R   **Realistic**—Is your outcome realistic according to you? It does not have to be realistic in the minds of others.

        Responsible—Assume responsibility for your actions and the consequences of achieving your outcome.

Y   **Yearning**—Without a real yearning or passion for achieving your outcome, it is only a series of words. Your passion will drive your activities and success. It will dominate your conversations, your thinking, your actions and your very being. To be passionate about an outcome, it must be in alignment with your values. You will fail to achieve an outcome if it is lifeless, too bland or one that someone else has imposed on you. In life, it is not necessarily the smartest or most gifted who succeed, it is those with desire.

Have a clearly stated, meaningful outcome for everything you do—meeting with your boss, family vacation or selling a product or service to a client, for example. How often have you not had a clearly stated outcome and, as a result, were co-opted to help someone else achieve their outcome? Afterward, perhaps you "beat up" yourself or them for being successful at your expense. To be successful, you need to know what you want, express it clearly and succinctly, be aware of the consequences and have a passion for achieving it.

> Twenty years from now you will be more disappointed by the things that you didn't do than by the ones you did do. So throw off the bowlines. Sail away from the safe harbor. Catch the trade winds in your sails. Explore. Dream. Discover.
>
> —*Mark Twain*

A MASTERY outcome can range from, "I will respond in a respectful manner to this e-mail in the next five minutes in a way that clearly demonstrates that I am concerned about this situation," to "When I meet with Bill this afternoon, I will present my five best ideas for increasing sales and request that he respond to each one by Friday of this week," to "It is now July 1, 20xx and I am earning $y per year in a career that fully satisfies my RIGHTS."

In section 3.2 "Know Your RIGHTS", you listed your RIGHTS for career, vacation, relationship, life in general, your next sales opportunity or something that is meaningful to you. Take a moment to review your RIGHTS for the situation you selected and create an outcome based on these RIGHTS that follows the MASTERY format.

My outcome is:

As a manager, consider establishing an overall MASTERY outcome for your team. This outcome, which should be known to all team members (even better if they helped formulate it), will provide the context for team meetings, performance reviews and handling specific situations. In a similar manner, parents can set outcomes for their family and family members that will guide how the family functions.

3.4. HAVE A BACKUP PLAN

Since people's needs and interests can differ significantly, there will be situations where you will not be able to fully satisfy your desired outcome and you will have to compromise. If you do not have a fully acceptable (to you) backup plan, referred to in negotiation terminology as Best Alternative to a Negotiated Agreement (BATNA), you may find yourself locked into your desired outcome with little or no flexibility. This could result in you rejecting a proposal that would be in your interest to accept or you might end up giving away more than you intended. In either case, this will not result in a win-win solution. A BATNA gives you the lower limit or walk-away point of your negotiating position. Your BATNA should also follow the MASTERY format, particularly with regard to ecology so that you are not taking this action to spite the other person or for the other person to feel sorry for you.

As you determine your BATNA, take into consideration the alternatives available to the other person. The more you know about his options, the better prepared you will be and a more realistic view you'll have of what the final outcome may be and what offers are reasonable. Quite simply, if the best agreement you eventually negotiate is better than your BATNA, then you should accept it. Otherwise, consider pursuing your alternative. If your BATNA is better in every way than what you could get from negotiating, save yourself and the other person time and potential upset by not engaging him in negotiation.

To determine your BATNA, develop a list of actions you might conceivably take if no agreement is reached. Explore how and if the different actions can be improved upon and what the reaction of the other party might be. Describe each option (different timeframes, locations, financing, etc.) in practical implementable terms and select the option that seems best for you.

An example:

> For a number of years, I have been delivering training with two business partners, who are also good friends.
>
> Recently, we decided to meet to discuss our upcoming training program. I really enjoyed doing the training with my colleagues, however there were a

couple of important changes that I would like to see and I was sure that they would also have some changes in mind. I took my time and prepared my RIGHTS. Based on my previous conversations with the others, I formulated an idea expressing what I believed to be important to them (their RIGHTS). It was obvious that there would be a need for all parties to compromise in order to reach an agreement. My BATNA was that, if we could not reach an agreement, we would still remain good friends with the door wide open to deliver the same or similar trainings in the future.

We are good friends, so establishing rapport was instantaneous. Then, because we trusted and felt safe with each other, it was easy to share our needs and to ask probing questions in order to gain clarity. After about fifteen minutes, it was clear that all three of us wanted changes that were not acceptable to at least one of us. After some discussion, we decided to put the training program on hold for a year. We spent the rest of our meeting talking about the things that friends talk about and ended the meeting on good terms so that any two or all three of us could easily initiate some other business project in the future.

Your BATNA will vary depending on the situation:

- A parent discussing with his child about helping with chores around the house may be very flexible in allowing the child to suggest possible chores.
- A parent discussing with his child her choice of friends and possible drug use may allow plenty of opportunity for his child to express herself to feel that she has been heard and yet be clear and firm on the final decision.
- A manager may invite staff input on how work can be done more efficiently and offer little flexibility on timeframes and expected results.
- A salesperson may see more value in having a client leave without selling his product knowing that the two have parted on good terms and that, should the person decide later to buy, she would contact him.

3.5. PROMOTE THE BENEFITS OF YOUR OFFERING

Win-win influence is basically, satisfying your RIGHTS while addressing what is important to the other person. In the next chapter, we focus specifically on the other person's needs and values (RIGHTS). In this section, we look at the benefits that your idea, product or service provide.

Have you ever mulled over a problem or issue and, after considerable thought, came up with "the solution," or at least a solution that works for you? What happened when you presented your solution to family members, co-workers, friends or clients without fully taking into account how they see the issue or how your solution will meet their needs? Well, I have and it can cause a great deal of upset. Quite simply, before presenting your idea, product or service to someone else, you must both agree that an issue needs to be addressed and you should have a good idea as to how your solution will meet his needs—e.g. what are the benefits to him?

Far too often, we think it's the product or service that people want to buy. In reality, however, people buy the benefit the product or service provides. Consider the following situation: you walk into a hardware store to buy a drill bit. Unless you are a collector of drill bits, it's not the drill bit you really want. You want to buy a certain size hole—that is, what the drill bit will allow you to do (a benefit). And you can even argue, it's not the hole but what the hole allows you to do.

> Bad sales people only know how to
> sell one thing—low prices.
>
> —*Mark Hunter*

The other day, I was listening to the radio and there was an advertisement by a local internet service provider (ISP). The ad began, "We have been around since the beginning of the internet, before online shopping, before spam..." As I listened to the ad, I thought, "So what! Who cares? How are you addressing my needs?" The company executives are well-intentioned and, I am sure, in the back of their minds, they have clear benefits associated with these facts. Unfortunately, I don't have access to what they are thinking. Their marketing staff certainly could benefit from the following exercise, which will assist you in gaining clarity on RIGHTS that your idea, product or service satisfies for the other person.

This company's advertising staff is not alone in trumpeting a piece of information or a product feature. Many of us have done exactly that to a potential client, friend, coworker or family member hoping that the person we are communicating with will see the unspoken benefit. Unfortunately, all too often, the recipient of the information does not make the connection to a benefit and only focuses on the feature, which does not generate a strong desire to buy but rather questions and objections.

Recently, my girlfriend and I were shopping for a washing machine. Comparing machines, I noticed that one cost $900 and another similar machine was $700. I asked the salesman, "What am I getting for the extra $200?" His response, "More features. For example, this one spins at 1,200 RPMs while the other spins at only 900 RPMs."

So What?

This exercise can be done by yourself. However if you have a friend assist you and you verbalize your answers to him, I believe you will get a richer understanding of the benefits of your idea, product or service.

First, let your friend know the role (client, family member, coworker) he will play for this exercise. Describe to him your idea, product or service. Then, with body language and tone of voice reflecting a real interest in what you have said, he says to you, "So what?"

Taking his response as a genuine expression of interest, you think for a moment and give your best answer, to which he says, "So what?"

Continue (at least four times) until you have identified really motivating needs or values that can be expressed in the RIGHTS model. Each time your friend says "So what," stretch yourself to find something even more motivating that your product satisfies.

You may decide to start this exercise by purposely describing a feature, with your friend replying with "So what?" Repeat this exercise for each feature until you have a good list of benefits that will meet a potential buyer's needs.

An example:

You are part of a work team and have designed a new database system.

You: "We have designed new software that we can sell to our clients."
Friend (playing the role of a potential client): "So what?"

You: "Well, it will allow you to share information about your clients with staff throughout your company."
Friend: "So what?"

You: "Instead of different people entering the same information on your clients more than once, each staff member can see what has already been entered, in particular any issues that have come up and been resolved or are still outstanding."
Friend: "So what?"

You: "This will help you provide a better and more timely service to your clients."
Friend: "So what?"

You: "Your staff can be more **R**esponsive to your clients' needs, increasing your company's **I**ncome, while enhancing your customer **G**oodwill, creating a **H**ealthier work environment for your employees through **T**imely replies to customer inquiries with enhanced data **S**ecurity."

I am having some fun here and I think you get the idea.

Now for a real example:

> Roger: "I am going to write a book on NLP."
> To self: "So what?"
>
> Roger: "It will deal with effective communication."
> To self: "So what?"
>
> Roger: "If people have better communication skills, they will be able to enhance their personal and business relationships."
> To self: "So what or for what purpose?"
>
> Roger: "They will achieve the results they desire."
> To self: "So what or for what purpose?"
>
> Roger: "To help others get what they want and create a win-win situation."
>
> And a title was born—"Win-Win Influence: How to Enhance Personal and Business Relationships (with NLP)." It was not quite that simple, but it does reflect many of the thoughts that I had when developing the title. Notice that I included "for what purpose?" as this may trigger different thoughts.

Through an exercise, such as the one above, you gain a better understanding of the needs and values (RIGHTS) your offering can satisfy for another person. Thus, you are able to present your idea, product or service in a way that is of greater interest to your listener.

Remember, the person asking "So what?" must do it in a caring and respectful manner—maintain rapport!

Your Elevator Speech

If you are in business promoting yourself, a product or service, or are pursuing a career or looking for work, you need to have an elevator speech that will capture the other person's attention and encourage them to want to know more. This brief introduction (about fifteen seconds or two sentences) conveys the essence of what you, your product or service does. Rather than a descriptive phrase about skills or features, it stresses benefits for the other person. This last sentence is easy to say, yet many people do not know how to separate features from real benefits. The "So what?" exercise can be used to determine possible benefits. Once you have a great elevator pitch, you will find many places to use it.

In addition to benefits, your elevator speech should have emotional appeal and include visual, auditory and kinesthetic words to help the other person, see, hear and feel your message. If you already know some things about the other person, you can customize your presentation to better highlight his specific needs or how he processes information. (More on this in the next chapter.)

Examples:

Project Manager: Through strong listening skills and an ability to grasp my clients' true requirements, I create and lead skilled and competent project teams that deliver win-win, on time and on budget solutions that address end-user needs. Problems are handled before becoming an issue, thus supporting the health and well-being of all involved.

Personal Fitness Trainer: I help my clients overcome obstacles and achieve their wellness goals in a healthy and safe manner through personal supportive coaching and custom designed fitness programs. My clients gain confidence and insights that establish a foundation for healthy living and for accomplishing so much more in life.

Take a moment and determine the real benefits people will experience from you, your business, product or service and develop a blockbuster elevator speech.

My elevator speech is:

4.

Prepare in Advance

4.1. OVERVIEW

You now know your RIGHTS and what you plan to achieve in your influence opportunity. Although some people will think they are ready, there is still much to do—e.g. where and when will you meet, how does the other person process information, what are his needs, what motivates him and are you mentally ready?

Good planning not only ensures the other person feels respected, there is the potential for a more useful interaction, a more qualified customer and a higher probability of success.

Where and When?

For win-win influence, all parties need to feel safe and be able to speak openly. Be aware that certain locations can be upsetting or have a negative meaning for the other person. You may wish to meet at a neutral or positive site and at a time when you both feel resourceful. Before having a critical meeting with someone, ask yourself, "For what I wish to accomplish, is this the best time and location for our meeting?"

How Do Others Process Information?

At any given moment, a person's five sensory modalities (visual, auditory, kines-thetic, gustatory and olfactory—the *neuro* of neuro-linguistic programming) have access to far more information than he can process consciously. These modali-ties (also called representational systems) are used to remember (represent) your perceptions of your "outside world"—based on the information you perceive to be important, of interest or relevant. For our purposes, olfactory and gustatory do not play major roles, while a non-sensory system (digital), which focuses on discrete words, facts, figures and logic, is quite important.

These representational systems play a significant role in a person's strategy for feeling comfortable and being open to seeing, hearing, getting a feel for or considering your idea, product or service. They are also important to his decision strategy. For example, a person who has a preference for visual will put more effort into looking for what they want. An auditory person wants to hear good things. A kinesthetic person will want to get a feel for it, and a digital person wants information that helps him to make sense of it.

To determine a person's preference, pay attention to the words he uses and his eye patterns—up (visual), one side or the other (auditory), down (digital or kinesthetic).

Unconscious Motivators

Meta programs are an important set of filters that determine how you perceive the world around you. Meta programs are deeply rooted, unconscious mental programs that automatically filter your experiences and guide and direct your thought processes, resulting in significant differences in how you communicate with others and the behaviors you manifest.

Early researchers noticed that two people with similar meta programs were able to quickly develop rapport with each other. On the other hand, if the meta programs were not aligned, people found it difficult to understand or agree with each other. Once you have determined the person's behavior patterns, you can choose specific words that will have the most influence on him.

The meta programs covered are:

Toward—Away From: Is the person motivated by goals and achievements or by issues and problems to be resolved or avoided?

A *Toward* person tends to be motivated by words such as: accomplish, attain, get, achieve, rewards, and they will speak about achieving goals, results and outcomes. While an *Away From* person would be motivated by words such as: avoid, steer clear of, prevent, eliminate, solve, get rid of, fix, prohibit.

Internal—External: Does the person assess his work through his own internal standards and beliefs or does he judge his performance through information and feedback from external sources?

An *Internal* person would be motivated by hearing: you know what's best, only you can decide, it is up to you, I need your opinion. An *External* person is motivated by what others think and will respond to words such as: according to the experts, your friends will think highly of you, you will be recognized for your efforts.

Options—Procedures: Does the person prefer to keep his options open and explore alternatives or does he feel most comfortable following established procedures?

Options people tend to use and are motivated by words such as: alternatives, break the rules, flexibility, unlimited possibilities, expand your choices, options. A *Procedures* person likes to follow the rules and is motivated by: correct way, tried and true, first/then, lastly, proven path.

Proactive—Reactive: Does the person tend to initiate things or prefer to wait for others to lead?

A *Proactive* person will respond positively to words such as: go for it, just do it, why wait, take charge, what are you waiting for. A *Reactive* person is motivated by: consider the following, let's investigate this further, analyze this, we need to understand this, this time we will be lucky.

Sameness—Difference: Does the other person look for things that are the same or different?

A *Sameness* person wants things to remain the same and is motivated by: same as, similar to, as you always do, like before, same except, gradual improvement. Words that will motivate a *Difference* person are: new, fresh, totally different, completely changed, radical idea.

Convincer Mode: How does the person become convinced about something (e.g. buying your idea, product or service)?

People are convinced in four different ways: 1. seeing, hearing or reading about your offering a **Number of Times**, 2. **Automatic** after processing a small amount of information, 3. is never fully convinced (**Consistent**) and you always have to prove yourself or 4. after a **Period of Time**.

What's Important to Others?

Prior to engaging the other person in a conversation, would it not be useful to have an understanding of his needs and values (RIGHTS) and how these can be satisfied by your offering?

Being able to look at a situation from different viewpoints can be very informative and can help you to modify and present your idea, request, product or service in a manner that is more acceptable to others. For example, a discussion between a mother and father over piano lessons for the oldest child may look very different from the perspective of the parent who values the arts, the parent who is looking for ways to save money, the oldest child, the other children or a non-involved friend.

The term *perceptual positions* represents a technique ideally suited to addressing these different perspectives, thus providing valuable information or insights into how effective your current communication methods are (including choice of words, tone of voice and behaviors) and possible alternative approaches that may yield better results. The four perceptual positions are:

- First position—your own perspective, filtered by your own beliefs, values and needs.
- Second position—the other person's perspective, taking into account (to the degree possible) his beliefs, values and needs, without, in any way, super-imposing your perspective. Some people have difficulty fully accessing this perspective, because "parts of themselves" creep in and distort the perception.
- Third position—the perspective of someone who is totally independent.
- Fourth position—the perspective of the larger system (e.g. your family, workplace, team). Taking into account the short- and long-term impact on specific individuals within this system can be very informative.

Get Different Perspectives on the Same Issue

Cartesian quadrants helps you look at an issue from different perspectives, while perceptual positions helps you view a conversation from the perspective of different people. Often you are limited as to what is possible or you stop taking action related to an issue/problem because you are looking at it from only one perspective. Instead, for an issue or proposed course of action, fully consider the answers to the following questions:

- What would happen if I did?
- What would happen if I didn't?
- What wouldn't happen if I did?
- What wouldn't happen if I didn't?

Once you have fully considered each of these questions, you'll have more clarity on your choices and possible courses of action.

Put Yourself in a Good Frame of Mind

You know your RIGHTS and desired outcome. You have a backup plan (BATNA). You have an idea of how the other person processes information, and how you might motivate him and his RIGHTS. Now to put yourself in a good frame of mind consider the following:

- Visualization

  Visualizing how you would like to see the event unfold, your planned actions and the other person's responses can help put you into a positive resourceful state of mind. Visualization is a long-standing technique used by self-help experts and coaches to increase motivation, reduce anxiety, improve interpersonal interactions and improve performances (athletic and otherwise). Many of us have used visualization in the past. However, often we have done it for something we truly didn't want to achieve; thus we visualized ourselves failing.

- Increase Your Motivation

  At one time or another, each of us has chosen or made a commitment to carry out a task that we are not fully passionate about or motivated to complete. Examples include, cleaning your office/desk, making "cold calls," or having that critical conversation with a family member, coworker or boss. A number of NLP processes have been developed for increasing your motivation and passion. Section 4.7 presents a process developed by Richard Bandler, one of the co-founders of NLP.

- Breathe

  Far too often, we hold our breath or breathe shallowly when in a stressful situation. Unfortunately, this only makes us feel more stressed. Breathing deeply in a slow, rhythmic manner acts as a mini meditation and can help you to relax and perform better mentally and physically.

4.2. WHERE AND WHEN?

In some situations, you do not have much say over the time and location for meetings or encounters (e.g. salesperson in a store who responds to customers as they enter the store). However, if you are planning a conversation with a family member or a coworker, or are a salesperson who visits customers away from your office or you are making a purchase, you do have some say over the place and time.

Create a situation where both of you can be resourceful, freely discuss what is possible and reach a win-win agreement that sets the tone for future similar interactions. To this end, you need to meet where both of you can feel safe and speak openly, to the extent possible. Be aware that certain locations can be upsetting or have a negative meaning for the other person:

- A venue that is foreign to the other person.
- A room where family disagreements often occur.
- The boss' office.
- The principal/teacher's office.

Venues such as these can be disempowering to one of you because they may arouse certain emotions or bring up past memories and thus threaten relaxed and open dialogue. When meeting with family members, staff or a client to discuss critical issues, choose a location where everyone can feel safe and speak freely. You may wish to meet at a neutral or positive site located outside of the house, work environment or client's location. And yes, there are times, for confidentiality reasons or to remind staff who is in charge, that meeting in your office is most appropriate. Before having a critical meeting with someone, ask yourself, "For what I wish to accomplish, is this the best location for our meeting?"

Timing can also be an issue. If you want to have a meaningful conversation with your spouse, you may be well advised to avoid immediately after he gets home from work and is in a less than resourceful state with many other things on his mind. Similarly you may want to avoid engaging a coworker when he is stressed trying to meet a number of competing demands. Recently I was in the market for a home renovation contractor. One company that I contacted wanted to send their salesperson at a time that met their needs and, in my opinion, with little regard for my time constraints. I chose not to do business with this firm.

4.3. HOW DO OTHERS PROCESS INFORMATION?

I am sure you have heard people say, "I would like see what you have to offer." "I would like to hear about what you have to offer." "I would like to get a feel for what you have to offer." or "I would like to make sense of what you have to offer." Each of these people is processing the same information in different ways—visual, auditory, kinesthetic and digital. Each of us has the ability to process information in each of these modalities. However, in a specific context, one or two are often preferred.

At any given moment, your five sensory modalities (the *neuro* of neuro-linguistic programming) have access to about four billion bits of information. These modalities are visual, auditory, kinesthetic, gustatory and olfactory. Kinesthetic can be external (tactile sensations like touch, temperature and moisture) or internal (emotions and inner feelings of balance and body awareness). The modalities are also used to record (remember) your perceptions of your "outside world"—the two thousand bits you pay attention to and perceive to be important, of interest or relevant. These recordings in your mind (pictures, sounds, feelings, tastes and smells) are called *internal representations*. Thus, the modalities are often referred to as *representational systems*—the primary way you represent, code, store and give meaning or language (the *linguistic* of NLP) to your experiences.

John Grinder and Richard Bandler, the developers of NLP, realized that we also process and store information in words, symbols and formulae. This sixth representational system is often referred to as "auditory digital," however the correct term is "digital." Digital represents a modality that is devoid of the senses and focuses on discrete words, facts, figures and logic.

Of the six representational systems, visual, auditory, kinesthetic and digital are used and discussed most often in NLP. Gustatory and olfactory do not play a major role and are often included with kinesthetic. However, if you are addressing an issue that involves taste or smell (e.g. food) or you are a person who uses and relies on your gustatory or olfactory senses to a large degree, these senses need to be considered separate from kinesthetic.

These representational systems play an important role in a person being open to seeing, hearing, getting a feel for or considering your idea and in his decision strategy for buying what you are proposing.

Preferred Representational Systems

You have access to information coming from all of your senses. However, depending on what you perceive to be important, you may focus on specific types of information, e.g. visual or digital. When buying a piece of clothing, you may focus on how it looks, someone else may pay more attention to how it feels and another person may be more interested in the cost and if it is machine washable. That is each of us has a preferred representational system. In general, one system is not better than another; it just happens to be how we are most comfortable processing information.

Your preference for a representational system may lead you to exhibit certain behaviors or characteristics. Before exploring these behaviors, note that, depending on what is going on in your life—the context—you may change your preferred representational system(s) from time to time. Hence, it is useful to notice the representational system others are currently favoring and refer to it as a current preference rather than limiting their potential by permanently labeling them as visual, auditory, etc.

The following are generalizations of the characteristics of people with a preference for visual, auditory, kinesthetic or digital representational systems. As with all generalizations, there are always exceptions.

Visual

People with a visual preference tend to:

- Be organized, neat and well-groomed. Why? Because they want to *look* good. And what do they expect from you? Yes, the same thing.
- Use *visualization* for memory and decision-making—often getting *insights* about something.
- Be more *imaginative* and may have difficulty putting their ideas into words.
- Speak faster than the general population. Why? Because they have a *picture(s)* in their mind and, if it is a moving *picture,* there is much to tell in a relatively short time.
- Talk about seemingly disjointed topics, yet in their mind they can *see* the *picture* that *shows* they are all connected.
- Prefer in-person interactions—to *see* the other person and his reactions.
- Want to *see* or be *shown* concepts, ideas or how something is done.
- Want to *see* the big *picture.*
- Forget what others have said, and become confused if they are given too many verbal instructions. However, if you draw a *map* or *picture* for them, they can *see* what you're saying.
- Remember faces more easily than names.
- Be distracted by *visual* activity and less so by noise.

Auditory

People with an auditory preference tend to:

- Be more aware of subtle change in the *tone* of your *voice* and more responsive to certain *tones* of *voice.*
- Perceive and represent sequences and are able to remember *verbal* directions or instructions more easily.
- Learn by *listening* and *asking* questions.
- Enjoy *discussions* and prefer to communicate through *spoken* language rather than the written word.
- *Talk* through problems and like to have someone available to serve as a *sounding* board for their ideas.
- Need to be *heard.*
- Be easily distracted by *noise.*

Kinesthetic

People with a kinesthetic preference tend to:

- Speak slower than the average person. Why? Because they need time to get in *touch* with how they *feel* about the topic.
- Be more sensitive to their *bodies* and their *feelings* and respond to *physical* rewards and *touching.*
- Learn by *doing, moving* or *touching.*
- Dress and groom themselves for *comfort* rather than for appearance.
- Make decisions based on their *feelings.*
- Stand closer to other people than those with a visual preference in order to *feel* the other person's *energy.* Whereas the person with a visual preference will stand back to observe more of the other person's body language.

Digital

The digital modality is devoid of the physical senses. People with a digital preference tend to:

- Have a need to make *sense* of the world, to *figure* things out, to *understand* concepts.
- Talk to themselves and carry on conversations with you in their mind. They may say they recall discussing something with you, when the conversation actually never took place. However, to the digital person, a mental conversation with you is very real.
- Learn by working things out in their minds.
- Lack spontaneity, as they like to *think* things through.
- Have *logic, facts* and *figures* play a key role in the *decision*-making process.
- Memorize by *steps, procedures* and *sequences.*

I have a PhD in statistics. Does this give you some idea as to my preferred representational system, at least when I was working on my PhD? Remember, I may have changed my preferences over time. If you said digital (facts and figures, logic), you are correct.

Can you see yourself in one or more of these representational systems? Does one sound better than the others, do you feel one is a better fit than another or is one more logical? A short preference test is available at www.renewal.ca/nlp11.htm to give you an indication of your preferred representational system(s). You can find additional information on the representational systems in introductory NLP books.

Knowing a person's preferred representational system and speaking and presenting your offering in this modality will help him feel safe and comfortable in your presence (rapport—see next chapter) and in getting him to fully consider and potentially buy your offering.

How to Identify a Person's Preferences

To identify a person's preferences, pay attention to the behaviors listed above for visual, auditory, kinesthetic and digital representational systems. Listen for the words he uses and watch his eye patterns.

What do you notice about the following four sentences?

- This product looks very good. I'd like to see how it works.
- This product sounds very good. I'd like to hear how it works.
- This product feels very good. I'd like to get a handle on how it works.
- This product makes good sense. I'd like more details on how it works.

The first sentence uses visual words, the second auditory, the third kinesthetic and the fourth uses words that are not sensory based (digital). Yet all four sentences convey the same general meaning.

The words you use reflect your internal thought processes. If your thoughts—your internal representations—are mainly pictures, you will tend to use more visual words when describing your thoughts. If the basis of your thoughts is logic—it is important for you to make sense of something—you will tend to use words that reflect the logic of your thinking. This is also true for auditory and kinesthetic. That is, you convey the form of your internal thoughts and thought structures to others through the words you choose to use.

The words a person uses provide you with an indication of that person's preferred representational system. The following are examples of visual, auditory, kinesthetic and digital words. This is not a complete list. Can you think of other words or phrases that might be added? Notice that some words like *fuzzy* can appear in more than one column.

Visual	Auditory	Kinesthetic	Digital
see	hear	grasp	sense
look	tell	feel	experience
bright	sound	hard	understand
clear	resonate	concrete	change
picture	listen	scrape	perceive
foggy	silence	solid	question
view	deaf	fuzzy	sensitive
focused	hush	get hold of	distinct
fuzzy	roar	catch on	conceive
dawn	melody	tap into	know
reveal	make music	heated argument	think
imagine	harmonize	pull some strings	learn
hazy	tune in/out	sharp as a tack	process
an eyeful	rings a bell	smooth operator	decide
short-sighted	quiet as a mouse	make contact	motivate
take a peek	voice an opinion	firm foundation	consider
tunnel vision	clear as a bell	get a handle on	describe in detail
bird's eye view	give me your ear	get in touch with	figure it out
naked eye	loud and clear	hand in hand	make sense of
paint a picture	purr like a kitten	hang in there	without a doubt

No matter what your preferred representational system, you use a mixture of visual, auditory, kinesthetic and digital words, and one or two of these will be used more frequently. This gives an indication of your preferred representational system. A caution: If I ask you a visual-based question—for example, "When you look at this painting what do you see?"—no matter what your preference, you will use many visual words. And if I am not careful, I may assume you have a visual preference when this may not be the case.

How to More Successfully Interact With Others

While the following example illustrates a romantic interaction, the principles are the same for other interpersonal interactions.

Think about a time when you first started dating your partner. You probably made certain you looked good by dressing and grooming appropriately; you and your date went to places to see attractions; you used appropriate voice tonalities and enjoyed the music; you touched and held hands; you made sure that you smelled good and visited different restaurants to taste different foods. In other words, you used all the representational systems to suitably impress and charm your date.

At some point, you moved beyond the "dating" stage and became partners or perhaps got married. Now, instead of using all the representational systems or sensory modalities, you and your partner may have reverted to the representational systems that you each prefer. And they may not be the same. If you are visual, you may want to get dressed up to go out and see a show, and expect and give gifts that are visually appealing—including the wrapping. If your partner, on the other hand, is kinesthetic, they want to dress comfortably, touch and hold hands, and give and receive gifts that exude a feeling. If you and your partner do not learn to express your individual needs and expectations in terms of your preferred representational systems, as well as show flexibility in satisfying each other's needs in their preferred representational system, you both may be in for a difficult ride. Has this happened to you?

Sometimes We Don't Speak the Same Language

Have you ever explained something to someone who responded with, "I don't see what you are saying" or "I can't picture this." What is at work here? One possibility is that the person is highly visual. You, however, have been using words other than visual; hence, your listener is having difficulty forming a picture of your explanation in his mind. And how do we usually handle this situation? We repeat the same words, only this time with emphasis, as if our listener had heard nothing the first time around!

Given what you've learned thus far about representational systems, how might you approach this situation differently so your listener can *see* what you are saying? One possibility is to use visual words to help him form a picture in his mind or you may wish to draw a diagram or picture.

Of course, it's not just visual people who may have difficulty with your explanation. An auditory person may say, "This doesn't sound right." A kinesthetic person may say, "I don't have a feeling for this." A digital person may respond by saying, "This doesn't make sense."

If you pay attention to the words people are using, you'll find they reveal to you how they see, hear, get in touch with or make sense of the world around them.

An exercise:
> Select a person with whom you are easily able to have a conversation. The next time you are speaking with them, listen for the type of words they use—do they use more visual words or perhaps kinesthetic? Based on your

observation, have a conversation with this person about representational systems and what they think their preference is. You may also invite them to complete the preference test (www.renewal.ca/nlp11.htm) to verify your assessment. Remembering that a person's preference may change depending on the context, explore which representational system(s) plays a major role when they are purchasing something.

Eye Accessing Cues

Have you ever noticed that people's eyes move when they are thinking? This is valuable information that can provide you with clues about an individual's preferred representational system. That is, is he thinking in pictures, sounds, feelings or talking to himself (digital)?

According to neurological research (Ehrlichman, H., & Weinberger, A. [1978] "Lateral eye movements and hemispheric asymmetry: A critical review." *Psychological Bulletin*, 86, 1080–1101), eye movement both laterally and vertically seems to be associated with activating different parts of the brain. In the neurological literature, these movements are called lateral eye movements (LEM), and in NLP, we call them *eye accessing cues* because they give us insights into how people are accessing information.

To understand how a person's eyes move, ask them the following questions (with their permission) and watch their eyes. Do they move up, down or to the side?

- What was the color of your bedroom walls when you were fifteen years old?
- What will you look like in ten years?
- What does your favorite music sound like?
- What would your voice sound like if you had marbles in your mouth?
- When you talk to yourself, what type of voice do you use?
- What does it feel like to be in a nice, warm bath?

Did you notice their eyes had a tendency to look up for the first two questions, to the side for the next two questions and down for the last two questions? In general, if they are forming or recalling a picture in their mind, their eyes will tend to go up to the left or the right; for sounds, laterally to the left or right; and down to the left or right for feelings or when they talk to themselves.

More specifically, if they are right-handed, you may have noticed the following (for people who are left-handed, exchange left and right in the following text):

- Question 1—eyes up and to their left. This is a question about something they have seen before; hence, they remembered it—visual remembered (V^R).

- Question 2—eyes up and to their right. This is a question about something they have not seen before; hence, they constructed this picture—visual constructed (V^C).
- Question 3—eyes on the horizontal plane to their left. This is a question about something they have heard before—auditory remembered (A^R).
- Question 4—eyes on the horizontal plane to their right. This is a question about something they have not heard before—auditory constructed (A^C).
- Question 5—eyes down and to their left. This is a question about their self-talk—digital (D).
- Question 6—eyes down and to their right. This is a question about their feelings—kinesthetic (K).

Note: The following picture summarizes the eye patterns for a right-handed person as *you look at them*. These patterns are fairly consistent across all races. For many left-handed people, the chart is reversed (a mirror image).

Looking at the other person

FIGURE 2: EYE PATTERN CHART

If you would like to have some fun, here are some other questions you can take turns asking one another—or you can make up your own.

Visual remembered
- What is the color of the shirt you wore yesterday?
- Which of your friends has the shortest hair?

Visual constructed
- What would your room look like if it were painted yellow with big purple circles?
- Imagine the top half of a tiger on the bottom half of an elephant.

Auditory remembered
- What does your best friend's voice sound like?
- Which is louder, your doorbell or your telephone?

Auditory constructed
- What will your voice sound like in ten years?
- What would it sound like if you played your two favorite pieces of music at the same time?

Auditory digital
- What is something you continually tell yourself?
- What are your thoughts about this book?

Kinesthetic
- What does it feel like to walk barefoot on a cool, wet sandy beach?
- What does it feel like when you rub your fingers on sandpaper?

For a beginner, I have given you a great deal more information about eye patterns than you need at this time. For the most part, notice if the other person's eyes generally move up (visual), to one side or another (auditory) or down (kinesthetic or digital).

People's eyes do not always move
Sometimes people's eyes do not move. This may be due to:

- The "look-to-talk" rule. That is, when you are making eye contact with some people, they will return your gaze directly, and their eyes will seem not to move, or move only very slightly and quickly. In this situation, they may be defocusing their eyes so their "internal" eye can look in the appropriate direction.
- Near-term memory. If the answer is something that is well-known to the person—their own name, for example—or is a recent observation, they will not need to search their minds for the answer and their eyes will not move.

Preferred Representational Systems

People's eye movements relate to their preferred representational systems. If you have a high preference for visual, your eyes will often go up to see images in your mind. Or, if you have a high preference for kinesthetic, your eyes will often move down to get in touch with your feelings.

And it is not quite as simple as I just alluded to. If your conversation is focused on something visual, no matter what your preference, your eyes will move up from time to time.

Remember, your preferred representational system is the sensory modality—visual, auditory, kinesthetic or digital—that you use to organize and understand some experience or situation. If I am speaking to someone and I notice that their eyes keep going up to visual, even if I am not using visual words or pictures, this is a clue that they may be forming visual internal representations; therefore, their preferred representational system is most likely visual. To assist them in creating this picture in their mind and for them to see my idea in a better light, I could use more visual words when speaking. On the other hand, if their eyes are tracking on the horizontal plane, this means they are processing in sounds, and their preferred representational system may be auditory. If their eyes move downward, they may be processing kinesthetically or attempting to make logical sense of what I am saying (digital). If, in addition, their eyes move downward to the right and they are right-handed, their preferred representational system is most likely kinesthetic.

Build Your Confidence in Reading Eye Accessing Cues

There are a number of ways to practice reading eye accessing cues. Here are two:

- With their permission, practice with your friends and family members. Watch their eye accessing cues and then verify your observations with them.
- Watch talk shows on TV (be sure the show is spontaneous and not rehearsed). This is a great way to practice—you can stare at the people on the TV and it will not bother them at all. Notice whether there is a relationship between where the person looks and the words they use. For instance, if the person's eyes are looking up, do they tend to use more visual words?

4.4. UNCONSCIOUS MOTIVATORS

Meta programs are another important set of information filters that determine how you perceive and make sense of the world around you. Meta programs are deeply rooted, unconscious mental programs that automatically filter your experiences and guide and direct your thought processes, resulting in significant differences in how you communicate with others and the behaviors you manifest.

Early researchers noticed that two people with similar meta programs were able to quickly develop rapport with each other. On the other hand, if the meta programs were not aligned, people found it difficult to understand or agree with each other.

An early NLP researcher, Rodger Bailey, determined that people who have the same language profile (choice of words, body language) generally have the same behavior patterns and vice versa. Hence, on the basis of the words a person uses, you can make predictions about his behavior. Also, once you have determined the person's behavior patterns, you can choose specific words that will have the most influence on him. Bailey called his set of meta programs the Language and Behavior Profile (LAB Profile). In this book, I have chosen to discuss six of the fourteen meta programs identified by Bailey. For a more extensive discussion on the LAB Profile, particularly in a business context, see Shelle Rose Charvet's *Words that Change Minds: Mastering the Language of Influence*, Kendal Hunt, 1997.

Some points to consider

- Meta programs may vary across contexts—work or home—and may change over time as you learn new information or experience significant events in your life. The meta programs you exhibit today or in a particular context represent a current preference.
- Each meta program represents a continuum from one extreme to another. For some meta programs, you may be positioned in the middle, between the two extremes. For other meta programs, you may be at one of the extremes. If you have difficulty imagining or relating to someone who lives his life as described by one extreme of a meta program, you are probably at the other end of the range. On the other hand, if you relate entirely to one of these descriptions, this is most likely true for you.
- When you communicate, your natural tendency is to explain yourself in ways that correspond to how you best understand or interpret the world (meta programs). Often this will not create any major difficulty. However, if the other person's thinking or experience of the world is significantly different from yours, communicating with him via your preferred meta programs can result in a communication disconnect, potentially making it difficult for the two of you to reach a win-win agreement. To have a meaningful conversation or relationship with a person who has different meta programs, you need to respect his model of the world, be flexible and speak to him in his language.

As you read the following meta programs, you are encouraged to identify your preferences and those of people with whom you come into regular contact—family members, coworkers, clients. Also notice how your choice of meta programs affects how you live your life and the interaction you have with others. Use this information to improve your communication and in reaching mutually satisfying agreements with others. In each case, I have described the extremes and it may well be that you or the other person is in the middle—exhibiting characteristics from both extremes.

The following meta programs are discussed mainly in terms of a manager influencing a staff member. The discussion is equally valid for a parent-child conversation or if you are attempting to influence a person to buy your offering. There is a wide opportunity for using this material.

1. Toward—Away From

Is the person motivated by goals and achievements or by issues and problems to be resolved or avoided?

Toward: These people are focused on their goals. They are motivated to have, achieve and attain. Although they tend to be good at managing priorities, they sometimes have trouble recognizing what should be avoided or identifying problems that can get them into trouble. They are clear in what they want. You will hear them use words such as: accomplish, attain, get, achieve, rewards, and they will speak about achieving goals, results and outcomes. To motivate or influence these people, use the words that they use in a context of achieving.

These people do not consciously look for mistakes. If a coworker has a Toward preference, his work may have numerous unnecessary errors, simply because he is focused on getting it done so he can achieve or do something else. In this situation, you may wish to point out that addressing his errors is a first step toward achieving what he desires. While staff with a Toward preference can benefit from the help of an Away From supervisor, this is the very type they will tend to avoid. Why? Because the Away From supervisor often tells them what may go wrong or what has to be fixed without allowing them to fully express their ideas on what can be achieved.

Away From: People in this group often see only what may go wrong in a given situation—they notice what should be eliminated, avoided or repaired. They are motivated when there is a problem to be solved or trouble in need of fixing. They are good at troubleshooting, solving problems and pinpointing possible obstacles because they automatically see what is wrong. They may set goals or priorities; however, they will abandon them immediately if there is a pressing problem. These people will tend to use words such as: avoid, steer clear of, prevent, eliminate, solve, get rid of, fix, prohibit. And these are exactly the words you can use to motivate them to get something done. You can motivate your staff who have an Away From preference by noting that doing a specific activity or achieving an outcome will help them to avoid or fix a perceived negative consequence. At times, your staff may be distracted and operate from a crisis management perspective as there are so many things to be fixed.

If you have a preference for Toward and your staff members have a tendency for Away From, they may find your behaviors annoying as you may be overwhelming them with things they can achieve, while not allowing them to fix perceived problems. On the other hand, if you have a tendency for Away From and are always noticing what doesn't work, you may turn your staff off as they may decide "Why bother? I'm going to get heck if I do this or if I don't."

To help you determine if a person has a preference for Toward or Away From, ask him questions such as, "What do you want (in a relationship, career, etc.)?" Or, "What will having that do for you?"

Toward buyers will be motivated to buy what you have if it will help them achieve what they desire in their life now. Away From buyers will be inclined to buy what will allow them to fix or minimize what they perceive is broken or wrong.

2. Internal—External

Does the person assess his work through his own internal standards and beliefs? Does he judge his performance through information and feedback from external sources?

Internal: These people have internal standards and make their own judgments about the quality of their work. They have difficulty accepting other people's opinions and outside direction. If they receive negative feedback regarding something they believe they have done well, they will question the judgment of the person giving the feedback. As a result, they may be difficult to manage. They assess information from outside sources according to their own internal standards. You can motivate this type of person with the following phrases: you know what's best, only you can decide, it is up to you, I need your opinion. For example, "I was thinking of doing (a certain task), and I would like your opinion." or "Here are some possible approaches. What are your thoughts?" Since they do not need feedback on their own progress, Internals tend not to give feedback to others. Thus, an External person working for an Internal person can feel lost without direction.

External: People in this group need to receive outside direction and feedback to stay motivated and to know how well they are doing. Without external validation, they may feel confused or have difficulty starting or continuing an activity. They may interpret a simple discussion as an order and then be overwhelmed with all you have directed them to do. They are motivated by phrases such as:

according to the experts, your friends will think highly of you, you will be recognized for your efforts, your teacher will be pleased to see how well you have done your homework.

To identify whether a person is Internal or External, ask them questions such as, "How do you know you have done a good job or this is right for you?" An Internal person may say, "I just know," or "It feels right." An External person may say, "My teacher needs to give me a good mark, say nice things or smile at me." And a person with a balanced Internal—External, may say a combination of the two.

If you are selling something to an External, he will want to know what the experts think or have there been consumer reviews. An Internal, will view expert reports simply as information and say, "I'll be the judge of that."

If a staff member has a preference for Internal, he will already know if he is doing a good job. Saying, "I know you are doing well," in a situation where he has decided he is having difficulty will most likely be greeted with an emphatic, "No, I'm not!" Here, you need to acknowledge his opinion and let him know you're available to help when he decides he needs it.

Staff with an External frame of reference will decide if they're doing well based on what others say. A well-intentioned manager may suggest areas for improvement without letting them know they're already doing very well. In this case, given the only feedback that they receive is about improving, they will assume they are not doing well. Give these people lots of supportive feedback.

3. Options—Procedures

Does the person prefer to keep his options open and explore alternatives or does he feel most comfortable following established procedures?

Options: People in this group are motivated by the possibility of doing something in an alternative way. They are the type of people who will develop procedures and not follow them. They enjoy breaking or bending the rules. Exploring new ideas and possibilities is of great interest. They may begin a new project and not feel compelled to finish it. To motivate or influence these people, use words and phrases such as: alternatives, break the rules, flexibility, unlimited possibilities, expand your choices, options. Listen for these words to help you identify this type of person. If a staff member has a preference for Options, make sure he has choices and that you are flexible (while still maintaining your standards).

Options-oriented workers are continually exploring different ways to do the job, and they learn best by exploring an idea from different perspectives. In so doing, they may never finish what they started. In some situations, they may need a little encouragement such as, "Once you complete this, you'll have the freedom and new knowledge to discover other ways to achieve what you really want."

Procedures: These people like to follow established rules and processes. Once they understand a procedure, they will follow it repeatedly. They have great difficulty developing new processes and feel lost without a clearly defined way to do something. They are more concerned about how to do something than about why they should do it. Bending or breaking rules is sacrilege! They are motivated by words and phrases such as: correct way, tried and true, first/then, lastly, proven path. A Procedures person will be more comfortable with routine and clearly defined ways to do things. An environment where the rules or ways of doing things are not clearly defined or changing will be upsetting for a Procedures-oriented worker, and he may complain that he doesn't know how to do what you have requested. If you are introducing a new process, preface it with, "We will be following a proven process for implementing this procedure."

This book is organized in a series of steps. Procedures people will easily relate to it and make it a way of life. An Options person, will find the material interesting, may follow the process once and then find ways to (in his mind) improve on it and do it his way.

To determine if a person has a preference for Options or Procedures, ask questions such as, "Why did you choose or do X?" Options people will give you reasons, while Procedures people will tell a story where things are sequential. Procedures people tend to hear "Why" questions as "How."

4. Proactive—Reactive

Does the person tend to initiate things or prefer to wait for others to lead?

Proactive: People in this group tend to initiate and not wait for others. From a Reactive's point of view, these people act with little or no consideration, jump into situations without thinking or analyzing, and bulldoze ahead with their own agenda. They excel at getting the job done. To motivate or influence these people, use phrases such as: go for it, just do it, why wait? what are you waiting for? take charge. To identify these people, notice whether they use short sentences with an active verb, speak as if they are in control or have difficulty sitting still for long periods.

Proactive workers rush ahead to get their work done. And it may be done without a great deal of planning or waiting for instructions. Here you may wish to point out (particularly if your workers also have an Away From tendency) that with a little planning, they can avoid unnecessary problems and actually accomplish more in the same amount of time.

Reactive: These people have a tendency to wait for others to initiate activities or until the situation is right. They may spend substantial time considering and analyzing without acting. They want to fully understand and assess before acting or they believe in chance or luck. They are motivated by phrases such as: consider the following, let's investigate this further, analyze this, we need to understand this, this time we will be lucky. This group can be identified through their use of long, complex sentences or incomplete sentences, use of the passive voice and nominalizations (the noun form of a verb, e.g. *communication* rather than *communicate*), use of conditionals (would, should, could, might, may). They will also speak in terms of outside forces having a major influence on their lives and relying on luck or the need to understand and analyze before acting. Reactive workers will delay, hoping to gain a better understanding before undertaking the assignment. As a manager with a Reactive worker, you may wish to give him a defined time to think about or analyze your request and let him know that you expect him to take action after this period. "Take until Tuesday to think about my request, and then we can sit down and discuss your thoughts and put a plan into action."

5. Sameness—Difference

Does the other person look for things that are the same or different?

This meta program actually has four different categories. For our purposes, I have grouped them into Sameness and Difference.

Sameness: People in this group want their world to remain the same or to change slowly over time. To motivate these people, point out how things have not changed, that they are still doing the same or similar type of activities. Use phrases such as: same as, similar to, in common, as you always do, like before, same except, gradual improvement. If your staff members fall in this group and you are moving to a new way of working, point out those things that will be the same or similar. Your role as a manager is to emphasize areas of agreement and how this is simply a continuity of previous ideas or information.

Difference: Change is a way of life for people in this group. They expect or will orchestrate major change every one to three years. Motivating words include: new, fresh, totally different, completely changed, radical idea. No matter how much things remain the same, point out all the things that are different, how things are constantly changing, and, if feasible, get them involved in planning and leading changes within the workplace. Staff with a preference for difference will learn best by seeing how new ideas or information are different from what they already know and will notice what is missing or does not fit. Your role as a manager is to show that what they are doing is new and unique. They can be the source of a great deal of frustration for a person with a preference for sameness because they easily spot differences and enjoy doing things differently.

To distinguish between Sameness and Difference people, ask, "What is the relationship between what you are doing now and how you did it last year?" Sameness people will say it is the same or focus on common activities or features. Difference people will highlight everything that is different.

6. Convincer Mode

How does the person become convinced about something (e.g. buying your offering)?

Number of times: To be convinced, some people (about 50 percent) need to have the opportunity presented a number of times. You see this often in infomercials—they offer a set of knives for $19.95. "But wait, during the next twenty-four hours these knives are yours for only $9.95. And that's not all, in addition, we will throw in a potato peeler at no extra cost." In this brief example, the knives have been presented to you three times. For someone with a two or three time convincer, he is motivated to buy if it satisfies his RIGHTS. Someone who has a four time convincer is not quite there, yet.

I am not suggesting that you follow this type of presentation. However, during your conversation with the other person, you can review your opportunity three of more times, and, as you do, emphasize a different need or value (RIGHTS) that it satisfies.

Automatic: A small percentage of the population are automatic. That is, based on a small bit of information, they infer the rest and decide immediately. These people only need to have the opportunity presented once and they are ready to buy or move on to something else.

Consistent: This is the group (about 15 percent) that is never fully convinced. That is, no matter how well you have performed in the past, you still have to prove yourself. In the past, you may have had similar discussions and they have always bought into your idea. And for them, this conversation is a new one, so you will have to convince them yet again.

Period of time: Finally there are people (25 percent), who only become convinced after a period of time during which they may gather and consider additional information. If the other person says they need time to consider your offering, respect their needs. You can, of course, ask how much time they need and ask if it would be OK to contact them again near the end of this period.

I have a combination of two of the above patterns. I like to see at least three different possibilities (e.g. if I am shopping for a laser printer, I need to see at least three different acceptable printers) and I like to think about my decision. If I have the luxury of time, I like to take two to three weeks and certainly would welcome and be expecting your follow-up close to the end of two weeks. If you show me less than three options or try to force me into making a decision now by, perhaps, offering me a good deal, you put me into an agonizing internal dance. I like the idea of a deal, yet want to see additional options and take my time deciding. On more than one occasion, I have walked away from a good deal because my way of buying was not respected.

An exercise:

Select a person with whom you are easily able to have a conversation. How would you rate them on the following meta programs?

- Toward, Away From or Balanced.
- Internal, External or Balanced.
- Options, Procedures or Balanced.
- Proactive, Reactive or Balanced.
- Sameness, Difference or Balanced.
- Number of Times, Automatic, Consistent or Period of Time.

The next time you see them; have a conversation about meta programs, what they think their preferences are and how you could use this information to make your suggestions more palatable for them. Remember a person's preference may change depending on the context.

4.5. WHAT'S IMPORTANT TO OTHERS?

> You can get anything in the world that you want, if
> you help somebody else get something they want.
>
> —*Zig Zigler*

Prior to engaging the other person in a conversation, would it not be useful to have an understanding of his needs and values (RIGHTS) and how these can be satisfied by your offering? Having an idea of the other person's RIGHTS can:

- Shorten the whole influence process.
- Provide a better understanding of how to present your offering.
- Lead to a better agreement for both parties—may give you an opportunity

to suggest something the other person forgot, did not think was possible or was out of his awareness.

- Avoid embarrassing missteps.
- Create a firmer foundation on which to positively conclude this and future interactions.

How do you gain an insight about the other person's RIGHTS?

- If the other person is a family member, friend or coworker, you have a great deal of information about his beliefs, values and what is important to him, if you just take a moment to think about it.
- If you are in sales and meet new clients on a daily basis, here too, you have useful information or can do a little research to get the information you require. For example, what are the current issues in your industry or issues clients may be wrestling with? What would a typical client be looking for?
- Taking time to assess the benefits delivered by your offering, may give you additional insights as to what could be important and motivating for the other person.

No matter what the context, you do have (or through some basic research can find out) information about the other person's current situation and hence appreciate his perspective and make a useful projection of his RIGHTS.

With an idea of the other person's RIGHTS, you can demonstrate how your offering does or can be customized to satisfy these RIGHTS. For example, I design and deliver custom training for clients. By having an initial list of my client's possible RIGHTS, I can make suggestions that will enhance the final product.

Effective influence is based on understanding the true needs and desires (RIGHTS) of the person you are intending to influence, and then presenting your opportunity in a way that is congruent with his indicated desires. People do things for their reasons and values not for your reasons and values. If everyone saw the world the same way with the same opinions and needs, there would be no need to influence as everyone would naturally be in compliance with one another. You may coerce someone into doing something you want simply because he has a value of not upsetting you or he is fearful of the consequences of saying no. This is not win-win and does not set-up future useful interactions.

Appreciate the Other Person's Perspective

Those in the service industry, such as waiters or sales staff, can have a significant impact on their own income and the success of their company by determining and paying attention to the RIGHTS of their clients. How often have you left a larger tip because the waiter made you feel welcome or did something extra that was appreciated? Or how often have you abandoned or thought about abandoning a purchase simply because the salesperson did not respect you or your needs.

One of my strengths as a consultant was being able to view a situation from the perspective of my clients and the system within which they were operating. As a result, I had a much higher success rate for having my proposals selected than my colleagues and my reports were well received by my clients and their management—even if they did not originally like what I had to say.

Getting different perspectives on an event or situation provides a more balanced approach to your thinking and subsequent actions. In situations where there is little or no understanding or progress, *perceptual positions* can provide a way of developing new understandings and creating new choices. The ability to experience yourself, your actions, opportunity and their possible impacts from different perspectives is an essential part of effective communication. These are the four perceptual positions:

- First position: Experiencing an interaction from your perspective. What actions can you take? How can you present your opportunity? What is important to you?
- Second position: Stepping into the shoes of the other person and experiencing (seeing, hearing and feeling) an interaction as if you were that person. To the best of your knowledge and ability, you take on the other person's beliefs/values, attitude, personal history and physiology and think in terms of how this situation would be interpreted from his perspective. Given what you know of this person, what is important to him? How might he interpret your actions (body language, tone of voice, choice of words) from his perspective? What is really important to him (RIGHTS)? You've heard the expression: "Before criticizing someone, walk a mile in their shoes."
- Third position: Standing back from the situation and experiencing it as if you were a detached observer. In your mind, you are able to see and hear yourself and the other person(s), as if watching strangers on TV. You act as an independent, resourceful third person and observe the interaction—the sequence of words, gestures, and expressions that occur in the communication—free of evaluation or judgment. You think in terms of what observations or advice an independent, uninvolved person would provide to the person who looks and sounds like you, in order to improve the interaction with this person.
- Fourth position: The fourth position is about ecology. This is where you explore what impact your actions or offering have in the short- and long-term on the larger system, including those people who are part of this system

and how the system may constrain what you perceive is possible. It gives you a different perspective on the other person's behaviors and needs. E.g. if this involves a family member, the larger system could be your family; if this involves a coworker, the larger system could be your work environment, including other coworkers; if this involves a sales opportunity, this could involve the impact of this interaction on your client's organization or your client's potential for referring friends.

Perceptual positions can be used with a past event to learn how you could have achieved a more desirable result (there is no failure, only feedback) or to notice what went well, so that you can repeat this in a future conversation. Perceptual positions can be used for an upcoming event to rehearse and get feedback on possible approaches.

An exercise:

Pick a situation in the past that did not go as well as planned (e.g. with a family member, coworker, friend or client) and for which a similar situation with this person or another person will present itself in the future.

Relive this previous experience from the following perspectives (be sure to clear your mind by looking around the room or stretching before accessing the next perspective):

- First position. View the situation completely from your perspective. Are there areas that need improving? How did you feel about being in this situation? Do you need to change how you think about yourself or the other person in order to be more successful the next time a similar situation presents itself? Clear your mind before accessing second position.
- Second position. To the best of your ability, take on the beliefs and values of the other person. Use this information to role-play. If necessary, have a friend coach you to take on this role by calling you by the other person's name. Sit, speak, and behave as he would. From his perspective, how comfortable was he in this situation? For him to be more open to the ideas of the person who looks, sounds and behaves like you, what changes would he like to see in this person? Take time to determine his RIGHTS to the best of your ability. To what degree did he feel his RIGHTS were respected and addressed? What would he like the person who looks and sounds like you do to help him get his RIGHTS met? What are his major objections? Clear your mind before accessing third position.
- Third position. To the best of your ability, take the position of an independent third party who is observing the interaction between a person who looks and sounds like you and the other person. What advice could

he give to the person who looks like you to improve the communication between the two of you? How could the person who looks and sounds like you better respect and address the other person's RIGHTS? Clear your mind before accessing fourth position.

- Fourth position. Notice the impact that the results from this interaction have had on the larger system—your family, workplace, etc. Is this what you wanted or would a different result have been more beneficial to the larger system? Not getting a win-win agreement in this particular conversation may have caused a little upset in the system. If this continues to fester (unresolved) for a month or even a year, what will be the long-term impact?

Repeat the perceptual positions exercise for a future conversation with this person. This time you incorporate any suggested changes that you identified from the above exercise into your approach.

- First position. Viewing the situation completely from your perspective, what will you do differently to get an improved result for both of you? What is important for you (RIGHTS)? What is your BATNA? What are you prepared to do to help the other person satisfy his RIGHTS? Develop as many options as possible to avoid being stuck. Clear your mind before accessing second position.
- Second position. To the best of your ability, take on the beliefs and values of the other person. Sit, speak, behave as he most likely will. From his perspective, how comfortable is he in this interaction? Are his RIGHTS being met? If he had objections in the past, are they being addressed now? Clear your mind before accessing third position.
- Third position. To the best of your ability, take the position of an independent third party who is observing the interaction between a person who looks and sounds like you and the other person. What advice can he give to help you improve the communication between the two of you? Clear your mind before accessing fourth position.
- Fourth position: Notice the impact that the results from this interaction will have on the larger system—your family, workplace, etc. Is this what you want or will a different result be more beneficial to the larger system?

Repeat the above, making adjustment each time, until you are pleased with the outcome or no new suggestions come to mind.

The more you can learn about the other person's RIGHTS, potential objections and how to handle them, the better prepared you will be to develop a more realistic view of what your outcome can be and what offers are reasonable.

4.6. GET DIFFERENT PERSPECTIVES ON AN ISSUE

Perceptual positions provides you with an opportunity to view a conversation from different perspectives; *Cartesian quadrants* helps you look at an issue from different perspectives. Often an issue/problem will limit what is possible or stop you from taking action because you are looking at it from only one perspective. *Cartesian quadrants*, based on the Cartesian co-ordinate system in mathematics, provide an opportunity to explore the issue from four different perspectives.

The process:

1. Be fully open to explore your issue and proposed course of action from different directions.

2. Relax and ask yourself the following questions one at a time, in the order indicated. Take time to fully explore each question and obtain answers for both the short and long term. If one or more of the questions seems confusing when you first attempt to answer it, relax and allow answers to come to you.

3. What wouldn't happen if you did?	1. What would happen if you did?
4. What wouldn't happen if you didn't?	2. What would happen if you didn't?

For example, if you have an issue about a change asked for by another party (e.g. spend more time with your family) you may wish to consider the following four questions:

- What would happen if I spent more time with my family?
- What would happen if I didn't spend more time with my family?
- What wouldn't happen if I spent more time with my family?
- What wouldn't happen if I didn't spend more time with my family?

You can be assured that once you have fully considered each of these questions, you'll have more clarity on your choices and possible courses of action.

4.7. PUT YOURSELF IN A GOOD FRAME OF MIND

You know your RIGHTS and desired outcome. You have a backup plan (BATNA). You have an idea of how the other person processes information (e.g. visual), how you might motivate him (e.g. Internal—External) and his RIGHTS. You are ready to proceed. Or are you? Far too often, we enter into important conversations without being fully prepared mentally. Feeling good about yourself and what you are about to do can have a significant effect on your success.

This section provides you with processes that will help to put you into a good frame of mind. For more tips in this area, I recommend a good introductory book on NLP.

Visualization

Visualizing how you would like to see the event unfold, your planned actions and the other person's responses can help to put you into a positive resourceful state of mind. Visualization works, yet how many of us visualize failing rather than succeeding? And then, after the fact, we say, "I knew it would turn out that way." Hello! You have just proven that visualization works, so how about visualizing your success!

Visualization and mental rehearsal is using your mind to experience working through an activity to achieve an outcome. It's more than simply seeing it in your mind—bring in sounds, feelings and, if appropriate, tastes and smells.

Does it work? There are many examples that show the power of visualization. Consider the following:

Australian psychologist Alan Richardson tested three groups of basketball players on their ability to make free throws. The first group was instructed to spend twenty minutes a day practicing free throws. The second group was told not to practice, while the third group visualized shooting perfect baskets for twenty minutes a day. As expected, the second group showed no improvement. The first group improved 24 percent. Using simply the power of the mind, the third group improved 23 percent, almost as much as the group that practiced. (Mary Orser and Richard Zarro, *Changing Your Destiny*, Harper & Row, 1989, p.60). Note: the participants in this study already knew how to shoot free throws. Visualization did not teach them how to shoot free throws; it helped them improve their technique.

The process (illustrated with the basketball example above):

1.   Make yourself comfortable. Relax and breathe deeply. You may choose to have some music playing softly in the background.
2.   Identify your desired, clearly described, achievable outcome—successfully shooting free throws. Often this outcome is a part of a much larger outcome—in this case, being a good basketball player.
3.   Close your eyes and create a picture in your mind in which you are about to shoot a free throw. Be fully associated (looking through your own eyes)

and see what you would see as you step to the free throw line with the basketball in your hand. Notice the feel of the basketball as you bounce it once or twice; hear the sound as the ball hits the floor and then your hand; hear what you're saying to yourself.

4. Take your shot, noticing what you feel, see and hear as you release the ball.
5. Hear the ball swish through the net and the crowd cheer and notice how you react and the feeling you get from successfully shooting the free throw.
6. Spend twenty to thirty minutes repeating this process, then again each day for a week.

Notes:

- For visualization to be successful, involve all of your senses. Adjust the qualities of the picture, sounds and feelings (e.g. make the picture bigger, brighter, closer or the sounds louder or more rhythmic or the feelings more or less intense) to make this experience as real as possible.
- You are in first position for this exercise and fully experiencing it from your perspective.
- Since influence involves the interaction with one or more other people during steps two and three, you may wish to briefly view the experience from second or third position. By doing this, you can assess the impact of your actions on others and how they may react, or you can give yourself some independent advice on how to improve.
- At the end of the visualization, notice how great you feel having achieved your outcome, and allow this feeling to move throughout your body.
- As with anything, practice makes perfect.

Visualization is a long-standing technique used by self-help experts and coaches to increase motivation, reduce anxiety, improve interpersonal interactions and improve performances (athletic and otherwise). The main reasons visualization enhances success and self-improvement are, visualization:

- Increases confidence—makes the outcome more real, more likely to occur.
- Improves motivation—as your dreams become more likely, you are more inclined to take action.
- Allows you to practice and test different ideas safely in a short period.

Many of us have used visualization in the past. However, often we have done it for something we truly didn't want to achieve; thus we visualized ourselves failing.

Visualization has the same effect as physically doing the activity
When you undertake a new activity, neural pathways are formed that allow you to repeat this activity again in the future. If the activity is discontinued,

the neural pathways begin to decline and eventually disappear. On the other hand, if this activity is repeated regularly, the associated pathways become well-formed, signals flow easily and the activity becomes a way of life or habit. Your brain cannot tell the difference between whether the action is physical or visualized. In either case, the neural pathways get activated and enhanced. This is an important concept that provides you with a means to develop new habits and to significantly change how you interact with others. To successfully use visualization to install a strategy or habit and instill it as a way of life, the key is to use and/or visualize the new strategy for five to thirty days.

Increase Your Motivation

At one time or another, each of us has chosen or made a commitment to carry out a task that we are not fully passionate about or motivated to complete. Examples include, cleaning your office/desk, making "cold calls" or having that critical conversation with a family member, coworker or boss.

The following NLP process can be used to increase your motivation or other feelings (or if you are a coach, those of your client) about a task that you have decided to participate in or complete. It is based on a process developed by Richard Bandler, one of the co-founders of NLP.

1. Check the ecology. If you were to be really motivated or passionate about carrying out this task, what are the possible impacts (in the short- and long-term) on those systems of which you are a part—family, work; on you or your health, etc.?
2. Create a task picture. In your mind, create a picture seeing yourself participating in the task or activity. Call this Picture #2.
3. Clear your mind. Take a brief moment to clear your mind of the thoughts from step 2 by looking out the window or noticing something on the wall.
4. Create a motivating picture. In your mind, create a picture where you are fully in action (looking through your own eyes, that is, you can see your hands but not the back of your head) doing something you really enjoy. Call this Picture #4.
5. Overlay the task picture. Re-introduce the task picture (#2) so that it is in front of and conceals the motivating picture (#4).
6. Create an opening (iris). Have a hole open in the middle of the task picture (#2), so that you can clearly see the motivating picture (#4) and you can feel all of the motivating energy emanating from this picture (#4). Make the hole sufficiently large to get all of the feelings from the motivating picture.

7. Close the hole and maintain the motivating feelings. Close the hole in the task picture (#2) only as fast as you can maintain all of the feelings from the motivating picture (#4).

8. Repeat. Repeat steps 5-7 as fast as you can at least five times, pausing between each repeat to clear your mind.

9. Verify that a feeling of motivation is associated with the task. See the task picture (#2) in your mind. Is this now motivating for you? If not, repeat steps 5-7 or verify that the motivating picture is truly motivating or that you really want to complete the task.

This pattern can be used in a variety of coaching situations. For example, if you are coaching a couple on their relationship, you may wish to re-install the passion/love they originally had for each other. In this case, the task picture would be one of their partner and the motivating picture, a picture of when they were truly in love with each other.

Breathe

People think they know how to breathe, yet far too often they hold their breath or breathe very shallowly. In a stressful situation, this only makes them feel more stressed.

Breathing deeply in a slow, rhythmic manner:[6]

- Acts as a mini meditation and can help you to relax and perform better mentally and physically.
- Helps your lungs and blood vessels function better.
- Helps improve the drainage of your lymphatic system, which removes toxins from your body.

The following exercise will help you breathe in a slow, rhythmic manner:

1. Lie flat on the floor. Take a slow deep breath—about five seconds to fully inhale. Lying on the floor for the first couple of times you practice breathing will help you to fill your lungs naturally, rather than simply extending your chest.

2. When your lungs are totally full, exhale slowly, taking about seven seconds to let all the air out.

3. Repeat.

---

6 www.realage.com/agingcenter/articles.aspx?aid=10487, July 2009

5.

Create a Space of Trust and Safety

5.1. OVERVIEW

Finally, you and the other person are meeting with the intention of reaching a mutually beneficial agreement—at least this is your intention. You have picked a site that is neutral for both of you, you are in a good frame of mind, you are prepared (know your outcome, BATNA, etc.) and you are committed to working toward a win-win outcome. You are on your way and there is still work to be done to help the other person feel safe, to gain clarity on his needs and to express himself clearly without fear of criticism or being taken advantage of.

Rapport—Establishing Trust and Safety

For most women, the language of conversation is primarily a language of rapport: a way of establishing connections and negotiating relationships.

—*Deborah Tannen*

Although you have an idea of the other person's needs, you would like to verify that these are indeed his needs and you would like him to listen to your ideas with an open mind. He will only do this if he trusts you and feels safe. That is, the quality of information he will provide depends on the degree to which you have created an environment of trust and safety or the degree of rapport between you.

So how do you create this state of trust and safety? Making small talk about something you have in common e.g. both play golf, only gets you so far and the other person may feel you are wasting his time. Instead, match his physiology, tone of voice and words he uses. For example, if the other person:

- Is sitting down, then sit to be more like him.
- Uses hand gestures when speaking, then when it is your turn to speak, move your hands with a level of activity that is comfortable for you and that is similar to his gestures.
- Speaks fast, then speak a little faster within your natural range. Similarly, if he is soft, loud or quiet spoken, emulate his speaking style.
- Uses certain words, use these words as well. Words are code meaning different things to different people. Using his words, lets him know that you understand his issue or needs.

There are also visual, auditory, feeling and factual languages that you can pay attention to. If the other person says:

- "I want to see what your facility has to offer." That's what he wants. Take him on a tour to see the facility, classes in action, workers on the assembly line, etc.
- "I want to hear about what your facility has to offer." That's what he wants. So talk about your facility in a tone of voice that shows you are passionate about your facility and its services.
- "I want to get a feeling for what your facility has to offer." That's what he wants. So give him an opportunity to touch/hold/grasp something that is relevant.
- "I want to make sense of what your facility has to offer." Surprise, that's what he wants! Provide him with facts and figures that describe your facility and services.

We tend to communicate and sell products and services to others according to what we would be looking for, not what our buyer is looking for. Be flexible and speak his language. In addition, to visual, auditory, kinesthetic and digital, pay attention to his meta programs. If he says he wants to achieve X (Toward), then this is important to him. Don't tell him how your idea will help him avoid or fix Y (Away From).

For an influence situation to have any hope of a successful win-win conclusion, all parties must feel safe and have a feeling that they can trust the other person and speak freely.

Pay Attention

Sensory acuity is a critical piece of any meaningful conversation. Are you paying attention to what is going on around you or inside of you? Are you consciously aware of the subtle clues that can turn a meaningless conversation into something worthwhile? Opportunities are available to make a difference in how you interact with others, if you take a moment to bring them into your sensory awareness.

When observing others, pay attention to:

- Words they use—visual, auditory, kinesthetic, digital and different meta programs.
- Eye accessing cues.
- Breathing.
- Voice quality and tone.
- Posture and gestures.
- Changes in energy.

This will give you important information on their preferred representational systems, what you can match to increase rapport and an awareness of when their thought processes may have changed.

The quality of your interaction with others is a reflection of your internal thoughts and beliefs. Listen to your internal signals when it comes to taking action, rather than doing what you think others expect or demand of you or what you have always done. Some of the internal or physiological responses to which you could start paying attention are:

- Holding your breath. When you notice you are holding your breath, take this as a signal to give yourself permission to breathe deeply at a relaxed pace.
- A tightening in your stomach or chest.
- A certain pain or twitch.
- A feeling of joy, love or accomplishment—or are these the feelings you tend to ignore?
- Internal representations (images and sounds) you create in your mind that play a major role in your subsequent behaviors.

Joe Navarro, a former FBI agent, has written a very interesting book on reading people's body language (*What Every Body is Saying: An Ex-FBI Agent's Guide to Speed-Reading People*, 1st Edition, 2008, HarperCollins). He recommends that you pay attention by using all of your senses. Indeed, the better you know someone (by establishing a baseline of their behaviors—how they normally sit, body language, tone of voice), the easier it will be to notice changes in their behaviors and what this may mean.

Acknowledge what they say: When the other person says something, particularly if it is an important point for him, you need to pay attention and acknowledge it. Not acknowledging the other person makes it difficult to reach a win-win agreement. You do not have to agree with him.

A caution: For sensory acuity, you must stick with what you have seen, heard, felt, tasted or smelled. You should not project an opinion or guess.

Psychogeography

Psychogeography is the geographical relationship (spatial and orientation) between two or more people. This has an important, often unconscious, nonverbal influence on the interaction between these people.

If you are facing the other person, this psychogeography will create and support a more direct or intense interaction (positive or negative). Whereas if you and the other person are sitting or standing side by side, then you are more like equal partners working on an issue or problem that is out in front of you and not seen to be "owned" by either one of you.

Change a Few Words

Sometimes changing just a few words can make a difference in how you and the other person interact and in what you see as possible.

Use care with negatives: A person's unconscious mind cannot directly process a negative. His unconscious mind first brings up the thought without the negation and then "puts a line through it."

Move from can't to possibility: *Can't* is a word used far too often. It shuts out the possibility of doing and achieving something. Change can't to "I haven't yet found a way to do xyz," this leaves the door open to finding a solution.

***And* is often better than *but*:** The word *but* has the potential to diminish or kill whatever idea, thought or experience immediately precedes it. Far too often we use *but* when *and* is a better choice.

Give a reason and get more compliance: Research has shown that providing a reason for your request can increase your chances of having it acted on.

Things to Avoid

Our intention is to engage the other person in an open, friendly, safe dialogue. And if we are not careful, we can upset this delicate balance. Here are some suggestions on things to avoid.

- Blatantly correcting the other person.
- Inferring there is something he doesn't already know.
- Telling him what to do.
- Passing judgment on him.

- Thinking he wants the same as you or has the same decision strategy as you.
- Being desperate to sell your product.
- Being unresourceful.

5.2. RAPPORT—ESTABLISHING TRUST AND SAFETY

The quality of information you get from the other person and your ability to reach a win-win agreement is directly related to the amount of rapport you have with him. Think about when you go to buy something; how eager are you to buy from someone you do not trust or with whom you do not have a positive connection?

In an earlier example, I talked about buying a washing machine with my girl-friend. In one store, the salesman was friendly, but he did nothing to establish a connection with us. After we left the store, my girlfriend and I remarked how easy it was for us to say "thank you" and leave without purchasing.

Establishing a climate of trust, safety and openness to explore your ideas and theirs is critical. After all, their ideas may add significantly to your proposal or may be quite different, yet deliver all the benefits you desire and more! Rapport is the foundation for any meaningful interaction between two or more people, whether it relates to a conversation with a neighbor, an interaction with your children's teachers, providing feedback to coworkers or concluding a sale. Rapport is critical for all you do, at home, at play or in business.

> Our most tragic error may have been our inability to establish a rapport and a confidence with the press and television, with the communication media. I don't think the press has understood me.
>
> —*Lyndon B. Johnson*

Rapport can be described in a number of ways. For me, rapport is about establishing an environment of trust, understanding, respect and safety, which gives all people the freedom to fully express their ideas and concerns and the knowledge that these will be respected by the other person(s). Rapport creates the space for the person to feel listened to and heard; it does not, however, mean that one person must agree with what another says or does. Instead, each person appreciates the other's viewpoint and respects their model of the world.

When you're in rapport with another person, you have the opportunity to enter his world, see things from his perspective, appreciate why he feels the way he does, and arrive at a better understanding of who he is. As a result, the whole relationship is enhanced and you have increased your chances of a win-win agreement.

Consider the following:

- Have you noticed how, when people enjoy being with each other, they have a tendency to use the same words and phrases, dress in a similar way or have matching body language?
- Have you observed that people who are not in rapport have differing postures, gestures, voice tonality and often avoid making eye contact with one another?
- Do you tend to gravitate toward people who have similar interests? For example golfers, people in sales, adults with children. Does your conversation become more animated as you share common experiences? As you discover more things in common, does the connection seem to grow stronger?
- Have you ever gone to a party or event for which the dress was formal, yet someone arrived dressed very casually? What was your first reaction? Did you feel that they somehow did not belong to the group? Or have you been at a restaurant and everybody at your table has been served their food except you? How did you feel? Uncomfortable, out of place?

The above points illustrate:

- The more you like the other person, the more you want to be like them.
- The more you have in common with another person, the stronger your bond is with them.

I remember attending a seminar by well-known NLP author and trainer Shelle Rose Charvet. She made her point on rapport very nicely with the following metaphor. If you are a bus driver and you are picking up passengers from the bus stop, you don't stop your bus a considerable distance away and then yell to them, "Hey, over here." You drive your bus to where they are and help them get on board and then you can drive them somewhere else. It's the same for influencing people: meet them where they are—in their model of the world—then you can help them discover new ideas and possibilities.

To create this state of trust and safety, match the physiology, tone of voice and words the other person uses.

Matching

The key to establishing rapport is an ability to enter another person's world by assuming a similar state of mind. *Matching* each other's behaviors, including body language (e.g. if his legs are crossed then, to match, you cross yours), tone of voice and verbal language—becoming more like the other person—is a powerful way to achieve this similar state of mind. Achieving a similar state of mind provides an appreciation for how the other person is seeing and experiencing the world (and vice versa) and creates an environment for reaching mutually supportive agreements. When seen in slow motion, matching (also known as isopraxis, postural echoing or synchrony) looks like a dance. If there is comfort between two people, you will see matching, accompanied by other comfort displays. When there is comfort, communication is more effective, we become more influential and transactions come about more smoothly.

Lovers can be seen leaning across a restaurant table, taking on a similar body language and tone of voice, as they gain more intimate visual contact. Indeed, one of the most powerful matching techniques is eye contact, whether you are lovers or have a business relationship. In a group of people (business or pleasure), you will notice those who agree with each other take on a similar body language, tone of voice and choice of words, while those who disagree will differ on these characteristics.

When two or more people have established a deep level of rapport (comfort), not only will you see similarities in body posture, breathing rates, tone of voice and choice of words, you will also notice that, if one person changes his body posture, the others will soon change to be more like the first person—assuming this person is what is referred to as the rapport leader. If he is not the rapport leader, you will see him change his body language back to what it was to be more like the others.

Reflective listening and feeding back a person's language patterns is a powerful way of entering and acknowledging another person's model of the world.

Consider matching body language first, then voice and finally the person's words. Why? Mehrabian and Ferris ("Inference of Attitudes from Nonverbal Communication in Two Channels," *Journal of Counselling Psychology*, Vol. 31, 1967, pp. 248–52) discovered that 55 percent of the impact of a presentation is determined by your body language, 38 percent by your voice and only 7 percent by the content or words you use. The percentages will differ in different contexts; nonetheless, body language and voice tonality have a major impact on your communication and ability to establish rapport.

Body language includes body posture, facial expressions, hand gestures, breathing and eye contact. As a beginner, start by matching one specific behavior and once you are comfortable doing that, match another and so on.

For voice, you can match tonality, speed, volume, rhythm and clarity of speech. All of us can vary aspects of our voice and have a range in which we feel comfortable doing so. If someone speaks much faster than you do and at a rate at which you would not feel comfortable, match this person by speaking a little faster, while staying within a range that is comfortable for you.

For spoken language, match the words they use. If the other person is using mainly visual words, you should also use mainly visual words; likewise for auditory, kinesthetic and digital words. To the extent possible, you should also use the same words as the other person. For example, if he is looking for an "awesome" solution, then this word is important to him and you should use it (but not over use it) in describing your solution. From your perspective, you may interpret "awesome" as "outstanding" and prefer to use this word. However, "outstanding" may have a different meaning or evoke a feeling different from "awesome" for the other person In this case, you would be mismatching, not matching, his words. If you have identified the other person's meta programs, you can use words that match those meta programs. For example, if you notice that he talks more about what he doesn't want or wishes to avoid than what he would like to achieve, then talk more about how your suggestion will help him to avoid those problems. Similarly, if the other person is looking for a tried and true process, then speak to him more in procedures language rather than how your solution is flexible and will allow him to keep his options open.

Some people find the idea of matching another person uncomfortable. They feel they're trying to fool or take advantage of the other person. To overcome this uneasiness, realize that matching is a natural part of the rapport-building process and that you actually do it unconsciously every day with your close family, friends and coworkers. Have you ever noticed that if a close friend uses a particular word or sequence of words that soon you, too, are using them?

As I was listening to the radio the other day, I noticed a good example of unconscious matching. Usually, there are two on-air hosts (a man and woman). The man has a very relaxed, calm, gentle nature to him and his co-host behaves in much the same way. That day, the man was replaced by an on-air personality who hosts a hard-rock show. Her demeanor is fast-paced and loud. Interestingly, that day the regular female co-host was also fast-paced and loud, and, at first, I didn't recognize her voice.

Does Matching work?
William Maddux at the INSEAD business school in Fontainebleau, France, explored the effect of matching on 166 students in two role-play experiments—one involved negotiation between job candidates and recruiters and the second between buyers and sellers (Maddux, W.W., Mullen, E., & Galinsky, A.D., Chameleons Bake Bigger Pies and Take Bigger Pieces: Strategic Behavioral Mimicry Facilitates Negotiation Outcomes. *Journal of Experimental Social Psychology*,

2008, 44(2), 461-468). In both cases, the outcome of negotiations was better for the would-be persuaders when they employed subtle matching. For example, in the buyer-seller experiment, 67 percent of sellers who matched the other person secured a sale, as opposed to 12.5 percent of those who did not.

The critical factors in matching are: be subtle, leave a small delay (two to four seconds) before matching the other person and, if you think your actions have been detected, stop. In all the years that I have been creating rapport through matching other people, nobody has ever accused me of matching (mimicking) them.

Practice matching with family members. It is a valuable skill for them to learn, as well. Have fun with it and observe whether they are aware of what you're doing. Notice how obvious you need to be before they detect what you are doing Start by matching one specific behavior; once you are comfortable doing that, match another. For friends, notice how often you naturally match their postures, gestures, tone of voice or words. Matching comes naturally. What takes practice is learning how to do it with everyone, not just those with whom you're already in rapport. In time, you'll find that matching will become automatic whenever you wish to deepen your rapport with someone.

An example:

Some years ago, I worked for a consulting firm. In response to a request for a proposal from a potential client, I followed up, did other investigative work and found out that, since this was a critical piece of work for them, they planned to hire one of the big six consulting firms. The firm that I worked for delivered quality work, but was not one of the big six. I knew my skills were ideally suited for this work and that I could put together a team as good as any other firm.

But how do I overcome their desire to work with one of the big six? One of the first things that I did was to invite the potential client and his team over to our offices for a lunch-and-learn, and for their team to meet with my team. Before the meeting, I coached my team on how to match body language, tone of voice, choice of words and suggested they ask questions and do more listening than talking. When the other team arrived, there were the customary handshakes and you could tell that this was mainly a courtesy visit. Before lunch, we had an informal chat with my team members paired up with theirs and matching physiology, tone of voice, choice of words and interests to the best of their abilities. When lunch was ready, my team guided whomever they were speaking with to the boardroom table in a way that their team was interspersed with mine. With my team matching those who sat next to them, very soon I noticed that the conversation became very animated and friendly. I concluded the lunch-and-learn with a brief presentation of the benefits (RIGHTS) my team could deliver and dovetailed these with what I understood their RIGHTS to be.

Because of the friendly animated conversation, the meeting ran longer than expected and I don't believe anyone noticed. As the other team left, the client approached me, profusely shook my hand and said he hoped we would bid on the job—that he looked forward to seeing our proposal. We submitted our proposal and soon after found out that we were on the shortlist of three firms for winning this business—us and two of the big six firms. As this had the potential of being a big financial opportunity for my firm, a senior vice-president decided to take over the project.

I told him about the success we had had using matching and suggested that we do exactly that when we orally presented our proposed work plan. He bluntly told me that we would not do any such thing and that we would present ourselves professionally as he had done many times when an executive with a major technology firm—a firm that was considered rather backward when it came to interpersonal skills. When presenting our plan, our team sat off to one side, not fully interacting with the client's team, the senior vice-president stood behind a lectern—sets up a barrier between you and your audience—with little eye contact, talked about the technical skills of the team (features) and spoke in a monotone factual manner. Several weeks later, we heard that we did not get the contract. I followed up with the client and discovered that it was a tough choice between the winning bidder and us—some of their team wanted us and others, our competitor. In the end, they decided that our team would have difficulty establishing and maintaining rapport with their staff. True story!

> The greatest ability in business is to get along
> with others and to influence their actions.
>
> —*John Hancock*

Experience the Value of Matching

To experience the value of establishing rapport through matching, consider the following two-part exercise. This is a fun exercise you can do with a family member or friend. In this example, let us call the two participants Ryan and Sarah.

Part 1. Ryan and Sarah select a topic on which they have a different opinion; for example, one likes broccoli, the other doesn't. Both Ryan and Sarah fully participate in the discussion. As they discuss the topic, Ryan deliberately matches

Sarah's body language, voice and choice of words. The conversation continues for about five minutes, after which they assess the quality of their conversation. Often what will happen is that, although Ryan and Sarah originally had a difference of opinion, as the exercise proceeds they begin to either explore areas of agreement or find that they have a much greater appreciation of the other's point of view.

Part 2. Ryan and Sarah select a topic on which they agree. As they discuss the topic, Sarah deliberately mismatches Ryan's body language, voice and choice of words (this time Ryan does not match Sarah, he simply participates in the discussion). The conversation continues for about five minutes, after which they assess the quality of their conversation. For this part of the exercise, it's not unusual for Ryan to become frustrated with Sarah and not wish to continue with the conversation, even though initially they had both agreed on the topic.

Examples of mismatching are: speaking fast or loud when the other person is speaking slow or softly, sitting differently, standing rather than sitting, not looking at the other person, using different words (visual, auditory, kinesthetic, digital or different meta program language).

An example of how not to conduct a sales opportunity:
Situation: A client walks into a car dealership.

Salesperson: Hello! Looks like a nice day.
Client: Yes, the sun is quite warm, yet the cool breeze on my face is very refreshing.

Salesperson: What can I show you today?
Client: I would like to get a handle on the cars you have.

Salesperson: I have many cars for you to see. I think you will like the new styles and colors.
Client: I really want something that is comfortable and hugs the road.

Salesperson: Let me show you this one. People will think you really look good in it.
Client: I don't care what other people think. I will be the judge if a car is a good fit for me. (exhibiting an Internal meta program response to an External meta program statement)

Salesperson: Isn't this one a beauty? The people who styled this really have it looking good.
Client: I don't feel you have the car that fits my needs. I am going to another dealership to get a feel for what they have.

Salesperson: Have a look at their cars and when you are ready, come back
and see me and I will show you a car that is a real beauty.

Here, the salesperson, who has a preference for visual, attempts to sell a car to
a kinesthetic client, according to his visual buying strategy. Although not fully
typical, many parts of this scenario are. And then we wonder why some people
just can't see how great our product is and how good they will look in the eyes
of others if they purchase it.

5.3. PAY ATTENTION

Are you consciously aware of what is going on around you or inside of you? Are
you paying attention to the subtle clues that can turn a meaningless conversation into something worthwhile? Are you responding to the opportunities that
are there—if you were to take a moment to see, hear, feel or experience them?
Are you listening to your internal signals when it comes to taking action or are
you doing what you think others expect or demand of you? Perhaps it is time
to begin paying attention to these signals.

People make involuntary movements or minor changes in physiology, most of
which they are not aware. Well-trained investigators are able to notice the most
subtle minor changes in people's physiology. Often, they can tell whether the
person is hiding something simply by noting changes in skin color (for example,
blushing, even for a second, is very noticeable) or how they move their body.

Sensory acuity—seeing, hearing, feeling (physically and emotionally), smelling
and tasting—is a critical piece of any meaningful conversation. When interacting with others or enjoying a moment with yourself, it is important for you to
be aware of:

- Feedback/information that indicates the extent to which you are on or off
  target in achieving your outcomes.
- Other people's actions and reactions to certain situations/stimuli.
- How you are reacting to certain situations/stimuli.

If you don't use your sensory acuity, you may end up far off course or spend more
effort than is required. For example, have you ever discovered after a conversation that you did not pay attention to what was important to a loved one? Or
perhaps you failed to heed warning signs and missed a potential opportunity to
establish a meaningful relationship or provide much needed support.

Often we pay attention to only what is important to us, through our preferred
representational system and meta programs, and we miss subtle or even obvious

clues that may be critical for achieving our outcomes, avoiding problems or helping others.

Observe Other People's Actions and Reactions

Whether you're having a conversation with your child, providing support to a friend, delivering a presentation in a business meeting, negotiating with another person or sharing an intimate moment with a loved one, it's important to understand how people experience the world around them. You need to recognize their meta programs and representational systems to more clearly express your ideas so they can see, hear or get in touch with your message. You should also be perceptive about changes in another person's physiology, tone of voice and energy that may indicate a change in his internal thoughts or emotional state. In these situations, you may need to stop what you are doing and alter your approach. Yet how often do you miss these signals and continue doing what you have always done, somehow expecting different results the next time?

When observing other people, pay attention to the following. This will give you important information on their preferred representational systems, what you can match to increase rapport and an awareness of when their thought processes may have changed:

- Words they use—visual, auditory, kinesthetic, digital and different meta programs (e.g. Internal—External).
- Eye movements (eye accessing cues).
- Changes in skin color and tone.
- Breathing.
- Voice quality and tone.
- Posture and gestures.
- Changes in energy—many people with kinesthetic as a preferred representational system or who are visually impaired are "highly" attuned to changes in energy. We all have the ability to do this; we simply have not taken the time to practice the skill.

Pay Attention to Your Internal Signals

Often we do not pay attention to what is going on inside ourselves. How often have you had an instinctive (body) reaction that said, "No, don't do this!" or "Yes, this is what I really want to do!" but you ignored it and later regretted your action or inaction? For some of us, the internal signals or physiological reactions are present, but we are just not aware of them—perhaps because we have ignored them for such a long time that they are now out of our conscious awareness.

Some of the internal or physiological responses to which you could start paying attention are:

- Holding your breath. Do you hold your breath when you are stressed? When you hold your breath, your body does not get enough oxygen, which causes even more stress. When you notice you are holding your breath, take this as a signal to give yourself permission to breathe deeply at a relaxed pace.
- A tightening in your stomach or chest.
- A certain pain or twitch.
- A feeling of joy, love or accomplishment—or are these the feelings you tend to ignore?
- Internal representations (images and sounds) you create in your mind that play a major role in your subsequent behaviors.

Be aware of what is going on inside of you. The quality of your interaction with others and your ability to achieve win-win agreements is a reflection of your internal thoughts and beliefs. If you do not feel resourceful or good about yourself, this will be evident in your conversation with others through your choice of words, your tone of voice, your body language and the energy emanating from you. Even if the other person is not consciously aware of these signals coming from you, he will sense them at an unconscious level and react to them in some way.

A caution:

For sensory acuity, you must stick with what you have seen, heard, felt, tasted or smelled. You should not project an opinion or guess. For example, you may observe that your child's lips curl up at the corners in the form of a smile, which is a fact. You may then tell him that he is happy, which is a guess, a hallucination or a mind read. The smile may be a result of the fact that he has any number of things taking place mentally or physiologically.

Mind-reading has the potential to get you into trouble. Consider the difference between a person when he is angry versus when he is very determined and focused on completing a task. The external physiological cues may be quite similar. If you ask this focused and determined person why he is angry, he may indeed get angry with you for making an erroneous judgment about him.

How to Read Body Language and Other Clues

What you observe in another person's nonverbal behaviors[7], can provide valuable insights into what is going on with him or her. Joe Navarro, a former FBI

---

7 Nonverbal behaviors include facial expressions, gestures, touching, physical movements, posture, body adornments and voice tonality.

agent, has written a very interesting book on reading people's body language (*What Every Body is Saying: An Ex-FBI Agent's Guide to Speed-Reading People*, 1st Edition, 2008, HarperCollins). Navarro says (p. 5), "One of the fascinating things about an appreciation for nonverbal behavior is its universal applicability. It works everywhere humans interact. Nonverbals are ubiquitous and reliable. Once you know what a specific nonverbal behavior means, you can use that information in any number of different circumstances and in all types of environments." I suggest to you that Navarro is stating this for people who are highly trained in reading nonverbals. My approach is not to be so definitive, but rather to stick with what I have explicitly observed and then get curious (by asking questions or further observation) to explore if the conclusion that Navarro suggests is actually the case in this situation. Later in his book, Navarro does say, "As with all nonverbal behavior, happy feet must be taken in context to determine if they represent a true tell or just excess nervous energy. Moving feet and legs may simply signify impatience."

Navarro recommends that you pay attention by using all of your senses. Indeed, the better you know someone (by establishing a baseline of their behaviors—how they normally sit, body language, tone of voice), the easier it will be to notice their nonverbal changes. Navarro suggests there are two types of nonverbal behaviors:

- Universal nonverbal behavior, which is the same for everyone.
- Idiosyncratic nonverbal behavior, which is a signal that is relatively unique to a particular individual.

According to Navarro, some of the nonverbal behaviors to pay attention to are:

- A person presses his lips together in a manner that seems to make them disappear. This is a signal that he is troubled and something is wrong.
- When suddenly caught in a potentially dangerous circumstance, a person may immediately freeze before taking action. That momentary stop is enough for his brain to do some quick assessing, whether the threat comes in the form of danger or something he forgot to do. Examples include: a person holding his breath or shallow breathing when questioned during a police or other tense interview, or momentarily freezing when the doorbell rings late at night.
- When confronted by a threat, a person will often fix his feet in a position of security (interlocked behind the chair legs) and hold that position for an inordinate period of time. To promote a win-win solution, you may want to encourage the other person to take a deep breath or to stretch or call a break.
- If the other person hears an unattractive offer or feels threatened, he may manifest blocking behaviors such as closing or rubbing his eyes, placing

his hands in front of his face, distancing himself by leaning away, placing objects on his lap, or turning his feet toward the nearest exit. Other possible blocking or distancing behaviors are not answering e-mails or telephone calls or a weak tone of voice.

- In response to an embarrassing or stressful situation, the other person may resort to calming or pacifying behaviors such as: gently massaging his neck, stroking his face, playing with his hair or exhaling slowly with puffed cheeks. Depending on the situation, he may resort to increased smoking activity or eating more food. These behaviors do not resolve the problem; they help the person to move to a calmer state so he can take appropriate action. When you see a person make a pacifying gesture, stop and ask yourself, "What caused him to do that? What can I do to help him feel calm or more resourceful?"

- A person will suddenly display happy feet (feet and legs that wiggle or bounce with joy) when he has heard or seen something of significance that has affected him in a positive emotional way. For example, think of game show winners or when a person is unexpectedly given something of value. They typically jump around. If a person is rocking up and down on the balls of his feet or walking with a bit of a bounce in his step, this may indicate being excited about something or being very positive about his circumstances. If a person constantly wiggles or bounces his foot or leg(s) and suddenly stops, take notice. This usually signifies that the individual is experiencing stress, an emotional change or feels threatened in some way. Desmond Morris (*Body Watching*, 1985, Crown Publishers) observed that our feet communicate exactly what we sense, think and feel more honestly than any other part of our bodies. In fact, your face is the one part of your body that is used most often to bluff and conceal true sentiments. While our faces can be very honest in displaying how we feel, they do not always necessarily represent our true sentiments. This is because we can, to a degree, control our facial expressions and, thus, put on a false front. Facial expressions can still provide meaningful insights into what a person is thinking and feeling. We simply have to be mindful that these signals can be faked.

- A person will tend to turn toward things he likes, and that includes individuals with whom he is interacting. If you join a group of people and they move their torso and feet toward you, this is a signal that you are welcome to join. If they only swivel at the hips, then they would rather be left alone. If, when in a conversation, a person turns his feet away, it is normally a sign of disengagement, a desire to distance himself from where he is currently positioned—with regard to opinions being expressed or he is late for a meeting.

- Leg crossing (sitting or standing) is a particularly accurate barometer of how comfortable (or confident) a person feels in the company of another. This body language is not used if the person feels uncomfortable. Leg crossing becomes a great way to communicate a positive sentiment (remember what was said about rapport and matching body language).

• Hand steepling signifies the person is confident in his thoughts or position. It involves touching the spread fingertips of both hands in a gesture similar to "praying hands," but the fingers are not interlocked and fingers on the same hand are not touching—the palms may not be touching. When a person's confidence is shaken or doubt has entered his mind, his steepled fingers may interlace as in prayer. Anyone intending to convey an important point should consider using steepling for added emphasis.

> The most important thing in communication is to hear what isn't being said.
>
> —*Peter F. Drucker*

We have focused on observing the body language of the other person. But what about your body language? For example, do you exhibit pacifying behaviors when you meet with another person or people? If yes, is there something you need to explore about your comfort in being in this conversation? Perhaps your posture and stance could be perceived negatively and put you at a disadvantage before you even shake hands with your client or say a single word. Influence is highly dependent on being seen as confident and capable.

In his book, Navarro suggests that nonverbal behaviors make up about 60 percent of all interpersonal communication. He describes many other nonverbal behaviors and provides greater detail on those mentioned above. If you are interested in exploring in more detail the validity of these and other nonverbal behaviors, read Navarro's book. He often provides a scientific explanation with appropriate references.

Acknowledge What They Say

I am sure you have been in a conversation where you have said something and the other person continues on with their line of thought without acknowledging what you said in any way. How do you feel? Do you think you have been respected and heard? I doubt it. And what do you do? Most likely, you stop listening to the other person and, at the first opportunity, repeat your previous point, or feel angry inside and look for an opportunity to end the conversation. Not acknowledging the other person makes it difficult to reach a win-win agreement.

When the other person says something, particularly if it is an important point for him, you need to pay attention and acknowledge it. You do not have to agree with him. You may say, "I hear you say … (repeating many of the words he used), I understand (or appreciate) why you think that way and I am wondering if you have ever considered … ?"

5.4. PSYCHOGEOGRAPHY

If you were sitting and speaking to someone who was standing—let's say towering over you—the potential exists for you to feel uncomfortable and not an equal partner in the conversation (mismatching physiology breaks rapport). In a similar manner, the geographical relationship (spatial and orientation) between two or more people has an important, often unconscious nonverbal influence on the interaction between these people.

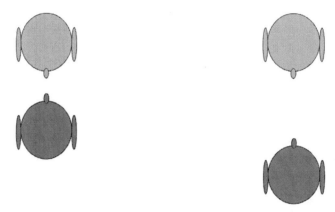

FIGURE 3: MORE INTENSE   FIGURE 4: LESS INTENSE
     INTERACTION   INTERACTION

In figure 3, the psychogeography will create and support a more direct or intense interaction (positive or negative). That is, it has the potential to enhance whatever emotion comes up—happy, excited, angry. If the potential exits for a negative interaction, you may tone it down by moving farther away, as shown in figure 4, or you may sit or stand at right angles.

In figure 3, let's suppose the purpose of the conversation is to discuss a problem. As the other person thinks about the problem, he may draw up pictures in his mind about the problem—potentially out in front of him, exactly where you are! That is, an association is created in his mind that links you and the problem together.

Now consider the arrangement in figure 5. These people are more like equal partners working on an issue or problem that is out in front of them and not seen to be "owned" by either one of them. If you are about to have a conversation about a potential conflict, you may wish to stand or sit side by side and talk about the problem out in front of you and how the two of you can work together as partners to resolve it.

FIGURE 5: EQUAL PARTNERS

Explore other situations where you have conversations with another person and the possible impact psychogeography may have. For example, one person standing and the other sitting, or perhaps a big desk or table that separates the two of you or you are standing behind a lectern as you deliver a presentation that is intended to be warm and inclusive of everyone in attendance. Are you creating the environment that best suits your intended outcome? Use perceptual positions to assess the impact of the psychogeography in these and other situations.

When having conversations with another person, remember psychogeography and pick the situation that best supports your desired outcome.

5.5. CHANGE A FEW WORDS AND MAKE A DIFFERENCE

Sometimes changing just a few words can make a difference in what you or the other person see as possible to achieve. It may be the words you say to yourself or to the other person.

Use Care With Negatives

A person's unconscious mind cannot directly process a negative. His unconscious mind first brings up the thought without the negation and then "puts a line through it." If I ask you not to think of a pink elephant, what do you think of? A pink elephant!

Notice how often you tell yourself what you don't want—"I don't want to mess up this sale." By expressing what you don't want, you raise awareness of exactly the thing in question and significantly increase the chances of it happening. Remember the law of attraction—what you focus on is what you get! Put yourself into a resourceful state by focusing on what you want.

The use of negatives has its place and, in some situations, can be used to your and the other person's advantage. Consider the following:

You are about to ask a family member to undertake a very difficult task. You could say either, "This task will be difficult." or "I *can't* say this task will be easy." Notice the different internal representations that each statement generates. Of the two, which do you think will be more appealing to your family member?

The other day, I was speaking to my daughter and inadvertently said "I will not challenge your ability to ….", which at a minimum raises the possibility of challenging her ability. Instead, I could have said, "I acknowledge your ability to …." For me, the second sentence is more supportive of her abilities. Fortunately, my daughter and I get along well, so saying it the way I did, did not cause any upset. In a different situation, it may have. So despite what I say in the book, I am still a work in progress and I'm continually paying attention and learning how to improve my influence abilities.

Move From Can't to Possibility

Can't is a word used far too often and it shuts out the possibility of doing and achieving something. If a family member, member of your work team or client says, "I can't do xyz," this closes down any possibility of him being able to succeed at xyz. If, instead, you coach him to say, "I haven't yet found a way to do xyz," this leaves the door open to finding a solution and puts him, with your assistance, on a path of discovery.

More specifically, if your child says he can't do algebra, what would happen and how would he feel if he talked about what he can do? "I can add, subtract, multiply and divide, and I haven't yet found a way to do algebra." This small change can have a significant effect on his attitude and how he feels about the task and his creativity.

And is Often Better Than *But*

You have just finished sharing an idea with a coworker and the first word out of his mouth is "but…" What's your reaction? Do you think he was actually listening? Do you feel he has rejected your idea without even giving it any thought? Now assume he said "and" instead of "but." Does this feel different? Do you have the feeling he was listening and is now building on your idea?

The word *but* has the potential to diminish or kill whatever idea, thought or experience immediately precedes it. "You did very well working with this client, but there are areas that need improvement." Far too often we use *but* when *and* is a better choice. Begin to notice where, in your conversation, you can enhance your communication by using *and* in place of *but*.

There are definitely times when *but* is useful. Here are two situations where you can use *but* to your advantage.

- You want or feel you have to declare something, and then would like it to diminish or even disappear from the awareness of those who are listening. "As a work team we haven't communicated as well as we could have, but that's in the past and we can do things differently now."
- You can use *but* as a pre-emptive move with someone who tends to respond with a "Yes, but." For example, let's say you want to present a suggestion to your coworker, who you know from experience tends to find objections or responds negatively to other people's ideas. You can say, "You may think what I suggest won't work, but I'd like you to fully consider it and let me know your ideas." If your coworker is someone who tends to take the opposite view, he will feel compelled to disagree with the idea before the *but*, particularly if you have a slight pause before proceeding with the *but* and the rest of your thought. This will tend to move him toward agreement with the second part of your sentence and be more likely to consider your suggestion on its merits.

Give a Reason and Get More Compliance

Providing a reason for your request can increase your chances of having it acted on. E. Langer, A. Blank and B. Chanowitz ("The Mindlessness of Ostensibly Thoughtful Action: The Role of 'Placebic' Information in Interpersonal Interaction," *Journal of Personality and Social Psychology*, 1978, Vol. 36, No. 6, 635–642) discovered if a reason was presented to a person when making a request, the person was more likely to comply than if no reason was presented, even if the reason conveyed no useful information. Although the research indicated that the reason could be trivial, I do not recommend this as it can quickly break the bond of trust and safety.

How often have you made requests without giving a reason? For example, to a coworker you say, "Please have this completed before the end of the day." Unspoken is, "because I meet with the boss first thing in the morning and this is something he wants to see." When making a request of another person, include a valid reason, rather than for example a parent to a child, "Because I say so."

5.6. THINGS TO AVOID

Our intention is to engage the other person in an open, friendly, safe dialogue. And if we are not careful, we can upset this delicate balance. Here are some suggestions on things to avoid.

- Blatantly correcting the other person. Sometimes he will make statements that are downright incorrect. If you experience this situation, avoid telling him that he's wrong or trying to overtly correct him. When you do, his defense mechanisms may automatically kick in. Then, instead of listening to you and being open to your ideas, he is now focused on defending his point of view. Obviously, this has a major negative impact on the air of safety and trust you have worked hard to create.

  When I was an executive in the Canadian Federal Government, I met with a salesperson who inquired as to whether we had addressed a certain issue. I proudly told him that we had and how we did it; whereupon he told me that we had addressed it completely wrong. I immediately stopped listening to him and showed him to the door well before our meeting was scheduled to end.

- Inferring there is something he doesn't already know. If you want to bring something to the table that he should have known, but doesn't, you may wish to start with "As you probably know …."
- Telling him what to do. Instead, you may suggest by saying, "You may wish to consider …"
- Passing judgment on him. If he makes a suggestion or answers a question inappropriately, don't pass judgment on him. Everyone views the world in a different way. His view may be very different from yours. Take the time to know him better and understand the basis for his view, including exploring his RIGHTS. In this way, you will be in a better position to link your suggestions to his needs.
- Thinking he wants the same as you do, or has the same decision strategy as you. Many people have difficulty with influencing others because, unconsciously, they tend to use the same strategies on other people that they would like to have other people use on them. We are all different, with different needs/values and strategies for buying a product or idea.
- Being desperate to sell your product. Some people resort to telling a client whatever they want to hear in an attempt to sell their product. Stop pushing your product in front of people. Take an interest in them instead of talking about yourself. The truth is, people are motivated by what's in it for them. Explore how you can help them. What do they need? Provide them with value that is important to them, yet costs you very little. Have integrity and do what you say you are going to do. Build relationships with people because, sooner or later, they will ask what they can do for you. As the old saying goes, "It's hard to say 'no' to people you know."
- Being unresourceful. If you find your energy depleted or overwhelmed, it is time to call a timeout so that you can recharge your batteries or assess all

the new information available to you. The timeout may be simply a bathroom break, taking a walk with the other person to get a coffee or leaving the meeting and the topic for several days. Continuing a conversation when you are not at your peak can result in saying something you may regret or agreeing to something that is not in your best interest. If you are feeling resourceful, but notice the other person is struggling or overly tired, you may take the initiative and ask if he would like a break to get refreshed and think about what you have discussed. Obviously, if he is not in a resourceful state, you have an opportunity to push your agenda and get the result you want. But it will be at the expense of the relationship and future opportunities to strike win-win agreements.

A growing number of studies show that making too many decisions or having too much choice can leave people weary, mentally taxed, and vulnerable to outbursts and bad decisions they might regret. By limiting the number of choices to evaluate, you can avoid the paralysis associated with decision fatigue. Having too many choices can lead to regret. If you choose something and it is not perfect, then it is possible to imagine that something else was better. (Decision fatigue can lead to unwanted choices http://www.canada. com/story_print.html?id=6029940, Accessed January 22, 2012).

6.

Understanding the Other Person

6.1. OVERVIEW

Imagine that you are a salesperson meeting a potential client, or a parent having a conversation with your child or a manager engaging a coworker about an issue in the workplace. You are in the process of establishing rapport or may already have done so (which is an ongoing activity). Do you know what is important to the other person? What motivates him? What are his potential objections? You may think so. However, I suggest this is an assumption that can get you into trouble. It's time to use the eighty-twenty rule—listen 80 percent of the time and talk only 20 percent. When you do talk, ask questions to find out what he is interested in, what motivates him, etc. Continue to probe until you have a very good idea of his most important RIGHTS, his preferred representational system, meta programs and possible objections.

> To listen well is as powerful a means of communication and influence as to talk well.
>
> —*John Marshall*

People frequently buy or agree to something because they feel understood by the other person.

Ask Questions

Nurturing relationships by responding to the other person's RIGHTS builds a solid foundation for current and future interactions and is critical to win-win influence. At this stage, you have a preliminary understanding of his RIGHTS based on your assessment prior to engaging in this conversation. Your task is to augment and modify this list, including adding major needs that do not fit the

RIGHTS template, by asking questions that clarify his statements, by seeking feedback and listening to what he says and how he says it (e.g. visual language, Options oriented). Updating your understanding of his RIGHTS and maintaining a space of trust and safety are two activities that continue throughout the whole interaction even as you are finalizing your agreement.

Everyone forms mental interpretations of what they desire. These interpretations can be formed in pictures, sounds, feelings, words or combinations thereof. Sometimes the other person is very clear in what he wants, other times he may have only an idea or notion of his needs. To be an effective influencer and set-up a win-win opportunity, your task is to assist him in describing his RIGHTS. If he is uncertain, assist him in gaining clarity, without imposing your needs on him. Once you both have a clear understanding of his RIGHTS and how they dovetail with yours, you can provide options and suggestions for reaching a win-win agreement.

Precision Model
John Grinder and Michael McMaster developed the precision model for gathering information in a business or influence situation, especially where it is critical to uncover and comprehend the other person's RIGHTS. The precision model is a series of questions that gain more information where there is a:

- **Lack of clarity on who or what:** The person(s), object or result to which the statement refers is unspecified or not clear. Possible question: Who, what specifically?
- **Lack of clarity on the action:** In this case, it is not clear how something was or will be done. Possible question: How specifically?
- **A comparison that is not obvious:** Although a comparison is made, what is being compared is unclear. Possible question: Compared to what?
- **Generalization:** Here a specific experience is generalized beyond what is fact. Possible questions: Everyone? Who, what specifically?
- **Limitation:** A limitations is a statement that is tied to your or other people's rules or requests that restrict what's possible. Possible question: What would happen if you did?

6.2. ASK QUESTIONS

Maintaining a space of trust and safety, you ask questions to gain greater insight into the other person's needs and values. The more you know about his RIGHTS, the easier it will be to address any objections, should they appear. For example, suppose he says that he needs "timely delivery." You have an understanding of what "timely delivery" means for you. But what does it mean for him? What are his criteria for assessing if he is getting "timely delivery?" To gain clarity, you need to ask a series of questions—specifically open-ended questions. "What exactly does timely delivery include?" is an open-ended question compared to, "Does timely delivery include same day service?" which is a yes-no closed-ended question. Notice you get far more valuable information with open-ended questions. If you ask a closed-ended question that has a high potential to invite a "no" response such as "Do you want to buy today?", then you may be putting yourself in a position that is difficult to overcome.

Good questioning skills are invaluable for salespeople, teachers, managers and parents as they provide a way to gain an understanding of what is important to those with whom they are engaging. A good set of questions provides a means to gather additional information and offers the potential of clarifying meanings, identifying limitations and opening up choices. An appropriate question asked with rapport can assist the other person in exploring other possibilities and interpretations, with the potential of seeing your offering in a more positive light. This is not about finding the right answers, but about aiding you and the other person in gaining a better understanding of his RIGHTS and how they dovetail with what you are offering. And it is about gaining insights on how to present your offering in a way that is most receptive to him.

> We are usually convinced more easily by
> reasons we have found ourselves than by
> those which have occurred to others.
>
> —*Blaise Pascal*

To know and understand the RIGHTS of the other person, you need to listen, ask questions and listen. I used the word "listen" twice as people are often telling us what they want, without our asking, if only we paid attention to them. Use the eighty-twenty rule—listen 80 percent of the time and talk only 20 percent. Listening promotes openness and acceptance. When you do talk, ask questions to find out more about him—what he is interested in, what motivates him, etc. Listen carefully, focusing on determining and satisfying his RIGHTS and notice if he is describing his needs in terms of:

- Visual, auditory, kinesthetic or digital language.
- What he wants or doesn't want (Toward—Away From).
- His standards or according to the opinions of experts (Internal—External).
- Keeping his options open or in terms of procedures (Options—Procedures).
- Whether he wants to do it now or would like to think over his decision (Proactive—Reactive).

- How it is similar to or different from what he already has. E.g. I want the same features on my new car as I already have (Sameness—Difference).
- Whether he wants to see several different models or needs some time before making his decision (convincer mode).

Having this information available to you and using it will assist you in maintaining rapport and presenting your product in a way that that is best suited for *him*—by using *his* words and directly addressing *his* RIGHTS.

People need to know that you understand their issues and that you can and are willing to help them solve their issues or satisfy their RIGHTS and reach their objectives.

As a former manager, I found it very useful to have an understanding of individual staff member's RIGHTS when engaging in performance reviews. If I have a good understanding of his RIGHTS, I can dovetail many of my and the company's needs/expectations and suggestions for improvement to meet his RIGHTS, thus creating a mutually supportive partnership. This is also a valuable approach for teachers, parents and coaches, when providing feedback to their students, children or clients.

Precision Model

John Grinder and Richard Bandler, the two co-founders of NLP, modeled two very successful therapists (e.g. Fritz Perls [Gestalt therapy] and Virginia Satir [family therapy]), who obtained extraordinary results with their clients by using certain types of questions to gather information. In this way, they and their clients were able to gain an understanding of their clients' deep issues and needs. As a result, their clients were able to identify fully acceptable courses of action and be fully participative in addressing their issues and making significant changes in their lives. This came to be known in NLP as the meta model. Although based on the work of two therapists, the meta model has much wider application—wherever two or more people are engaged in communicating—at work or at play.

John Grinder and Michael McMaster (*Precision: A New Approach to Communication: How to Get the Information You Need to Get Results*, Grinder, DeLozier & Associates, 1994) developed the precision model, a subset of the meta model questions, for gathering information in a business or influence situation, especially where it is critical to uncover and comprehend the other person's RIGHTS.

Once mastered, the precision model is a powerful and useful tool. However, it does take practice to master the questioning process. It must be undertaken with a high degree of rapport—the other person must feel safe and not pressured—and used with moderation. Before asking any of my clients, students or family members meta or precision model questions, I make sure that they are comfortable in my presence and have a feeling of security. I often start with the following: "May I ask you a question?" If they respond negatively, I do not pursue it. Instead, I listen to their use of visual, auditory, kinesthetic and digital words and identify different meta programs in their choice of words to get a clearer understanding of how they experience the world and the issue they are wrestling with.

Precision Model Examples

Lack of clarity on who or what.

The person, object or result to which the statement refers is unspecified or not clear.

Words that indicate this situation are: we, they, friends, teachers, school, people.

Example	Questions to recover lost information
He doesn't like my house.	Who specifically? What specifically does he not like?

Lack of clarity on the action.

In this case, it is not clear how something was or will be done.

Example	Questions to recover lost information
I need to improve how I talk to people.	How specifically are you going to improve how you talk to people?

Comparison is not obvious

Although a comparison is made, what is being compared is unclear. The sentence will often contain words such as: good, bad, better, best, worst, more, less, most, least, few, improved, great, newer.

Example	Questions to recover lost information
Your offer needs to be better.	Compared to what? How specifically?

Generalization

Here a specific experience is generalized beyond what is fact. Words that indicate this are: all, everyone, nobody, every, never, always. To address generalizations, emphasize the generalization or provide a counter example.

Example	Questions to recover lost information
Staff say this is what we should do.	All the staff? Who specifically?
Nobody thinks this is a good idea.	Nobody? Who specifically?
I never get recognized for my contribution to the team.	Did I not praise you during the last team meeting?

Limitations

Limitations are statements that are tied to your or other people's rules or requests that restrict what is possible. Words that indicate this are: can/can't, possible/impossible, should/shouldn't, must/mustn't, have to, need to, necessary.

Example	Questions to recover lost information
I can't get my work done in this environment.	What stops you?
I shouldn't buy it now.	What would happen if you did?

In the above examples and in real life, you could ask several different questions. Which question you begin with depends on which aspect of what the other person has said will give you the most clarity on his RIGHTS, motivation or possible objections.

As a first step in learning how to use the precision model, I suggest you take time to identify the patterns in your own conversations and practice developing the questions that recover the lost information. You may wish to write a few paragraphs about your career, your family or your views of life. Then identify the precision model patterns and corresponding questions. Make sure you honestly answer these questions and notice if new understandings or possibilities are opened up.

Ask "How?" rather than "Why?"

Notice that none of the questions in the precision model begins with "why." When you ask someone a "why" question, often he may feel he has to defend what he has said or done, make excuses or rationalize his behavior. This provides little potential for gaining clarity on his RIGHTS or how to resolve an issue. Asking "how" gives you an understanding of the process and "how" the problem arose and thus more information; for example, "How has this become a problem for you?"

An example:

This is a clearly fictitious example to illustrate the precision model and other points covered in this book.

Situation: A client walks into a car dealership. (By this time, the salesperson has read my book and knows that he needs to gain information on the other person's needs. He is also better at identifying the preferred representational system of his client. Can you? Hint: It's not the kinesthetic client as he never came back.)

Salesperson: Good morning. Looks like a nice day.
Client: Yes, the temperature should be in the mid 70s today.

Salesperson: Is there something I can interest you in?
Client: Yes, I would like to get some information.

Salesperson: Specifically, what type of information?
Client: Safety features (S), reliability (R), guarantee (G) are most important to me. I am always concerned about cost (Investment [I]) and I want to purchase it this week (Time [T]).

Salesperson: How about this model here. Great safety record, proven reliability. Has a five year best in its class warrantee, has the lowest operating costs of comparable cars, is less than $20,000 and is available now.
Client: People say that car has a poor repair record.

Salesman: Who specifically says that?
Client: My grandfather, he owned one fifteen years ago.

Salesperson: Your grandfather is correct about this car fifteen years ago. This manufacturer recognized their mistakes and put a great deal of effort in correcting them. Here are the details on the latest model in *Consumer Reports.*
Client: That's great. I will purchase this model.

Salesperson: Shall I have it available for you tomorrow?
Client: I can't pick it up tomorrow.

Salesperson: What stops you?
Client: I don't have any convenient way to get here tomorrow.

Salesperson: Where do you live? Perhaps I can pick you up, if that's OK.
Client: Fantastic. You have really been helpful (H). That's important to me. I will refer you to my friends.

Sometimes It's Not That Simple

The other person doesn't want to be questioned

The other person may not want to answer your questions for several reasons:

- You have not established rapport.
- The context or current situation reminds him of a similar past event that didn't go very well.
- He tends to approach a buying situation as a skeptic.

Nonetheless, he is still engaging you in conversation because he wants access to the information you have and wants to thoroughly assess it before making any decisions—potentially without you trying to sell him.

You need to respect his needs, while still guiding the conversation. Rather than asking your usual set of questions to uncover his RIGHTS, make it clear that the questions you are asking will help you to provide him with the information he needs to make the best decision. Changing tactics and depending on the context, you may say, "I can present a number of different options to you, each addressing different needs and I want to make sure that I meet your needs to the best degree possible. Would you say your primary need is R, G or H?" (drawing on your preliminary assessment of his or a similar client's potential RIGHTS). If possible, ask at least four questions like this. The more questions he answers, the easier it becomes to eventually ask the open-ended questions that will allow you to gain more clarity on his RIGHTS.

Solution needs a problem to address

In sales, you only have a solution if the other person knows there is a problem to be addressed. Telling him that he has a problem and you have the solution is seldom a winning strategy. In this situation, your role is to help him identify and define the problem that needs to be addressed.

If you are selling a product or service in a specific industry, you have a pretty good understanding of the issues facing your client. You may wish to start the conversation by saying, "I understand that in our industry, organizations are faced with three major problems—X, Y and Z. Do you agree? Has your organization faced these issues and how have you addressed them?" If he has already been working on one of these problems, he has an opportunity to brag about how he is addressing it and potentially where he may need some assistance. You may have raised a problem that he was not aware of and may reply to you, "I was not aware of Z, how are other organizations addressing this?" And he may try to one-up you by raising other problems that are facing him. Now you have the opportunity through good questioning, such as the precision model, to find out what his RIGHTS are and how your product can best address these.

Sometimes clients have the solution

As a consultant, I have been in situations where my potential client has already identified the solution to his issue. Sometimes he has clearly identified the issue and developed a great solution. However, what about those situations where the solution is lacking or the issue is poorly or narrowly defined?

Consider the situation where the issue is well defined but the solution is lacking. Since the issue is well defined, there should be a good understanding of the needs and values (RIGHTS) that are to be addressed. Determine the RIGHTS that the proposed solution addresses, compare the two and notice how well they match. If there is a significant gap, you can now engage your client in looking at alternative solutions.

If there is a question as to how well the issue has been defined, you may wish to explore answers to the question, "This is a solution to what problem?" In NLP jargon, this is called *chunking up*. In other words, you are moving to bigger more general chunks of information. The context will determine how and which questions you will use. Here are two basic questions you can use to move to more general or abstract information:

- What is this an example of or part of?
- What is the intention or purpose?

The "So What" exercise in section 3.5 is an example of chunking up.

For example, suppose your client decides he needs a three-day course for staff to improve customer service. You may think, *What is this an example of or part of?* You explore this avenue of questioning and discover there is a larger training initiative to upgrade staff skills. You explore this further and propose a more focused and cost-effective two-day program that fully integrates with and supports the larger training initiative, thus satisfying more of your client's RIGHTS.

Or for the same situation, with rapport, you ask your client, "What is the intention or purpose of this initiative?" You find out that management is upset about the company's poor customer service record and wants significant changes now. So how can customer service be improved? Training is one possibility. However other possibilities are to modify procedures (including reporting responsibilities), acquire additional staff, change the physical location of where customer service is delivered, contract out some of the duties, etc. Now, depending on your clients RIGHTS, you have a real opportunity to deliver something worthwhile.

For a non-business example, let's suppose your spouse comes to you and says, "I think we should buy bicycles for each of us." Now this idea (a solution to what problem?) comes to you out of the blue. You could argue about whether or not you should buy bicycles, which would not be a great deal of fun. Instead, you may think, *My spouse obviously has a good reason for this suggestion, so let me find out what it is.* You may wish to be diplomatic and say, "I'm curious, what has led you to this interesting idea? If we were to buy bicycles, what would this allow us to do?"

He might reply, "We could go for bicycle rides on the bicycle pathways."

"For what purpose?" you ask with love and caring.
"To get some exercise, while experiencing nature," he says.

"For what purpose?" you inquire.
He responds, with love in his voice, "To do things together."

At this point, you may choose to stop and agree that purchasing bicycles is a great idea. Or you may pick up on the idea that your spouse would like to do things together that have a nature experience and involve some form of activity. And you agree that this is a great idea, as well. Can you think of any other possibilities if riding a bicycle is not for you? How about hiking, canoeing, horseback riding, golf? Strive to choose something you and your spouse both like, thus avoiding an unnecessary argument.

Determine how your client likes to buy
People tend to buy in the same way they have purchased similar items in the past. As part of determining the other person's RIGHTS, you can inquire if he has ever purchased a similar product. If yes, and he was happy with his purchase, ask him to describe the process, if he prefers to follow that process this time and what was important (RIGHTS) to him.

If you work for someone and, as part of your duties you need to present him with reports or other products, pay attention to how he likes to receive this type of product. Then say to him, "I want to do the best job that I can for you and I would like to work in a way that supports how you like to do business. You expect me to provide you with information/advice so that you can make a decision. Would you prefer to see this information in a report, have a discussion about it, get a feel for it by working through it, receive facts and figures or some combination thereof?" You can then explore whether he is more Toward—Away From, Internal—External, etc.

Your client may express his needs in terms of what he doesn't want (Away From). If he talks about what he does want (Toward), this is easier as you and he know what is expected. When he says, "I don't want the room painted blue," until you ask more questions, any other color will do. Unfortunately, in these types of situations, some of us don't ask questions and guess at what "I don't want X" means and hope that our guess is correct. Asking questions such as, "If you don't want X, what do you want? How will you know if you have achieved it?" will give you an opportunity to gain more clarity on his RIGHTS.

Make sure you are negotiating with the right person—one who can make a decision

Negotiating with someone who does not have authority to make a buying decision can be a major problem. You spend a great deal of time and energy negotiating in good faith and strike a tentative deal and then your client says, "I will have to run this by my manager." This is an annoying tactic used by some car dealerships.

If in doubt, before beginning any meaningful conversation, ask a question such as: "If we discuss this and we decide that we can reach an agreement, will you need to consult someone else to get their approval, or are you able to make that decision yourself today?" If the approval of another person is required, that person should be present during the discussion.

7.

Bridge the Gap

7.1. OVERVIEW

As the saying goes, "Everything you have learned so far still counts."

Although the activities of chapters five, six and seven have a natural flow, one to the other, these activities most likely will be implemented concurrently and provide valuable information that supports the efficacy of the others.

You have an understanding of the other person's RIGHTS and how these dovetail with your offering. And there is a gap which initially could be quite large. You now explore how to close this gap in a respectful manner that takes the client's needs into account. Often you do not have to satisfy all of other person's RIGHTS. However, the more you do, the more likely you will get an agreement.

There are four steps to bridging the gap:

- Identify current choice.
- Doubt or question current choice.
- Explore alternatives.
- Confirm new choice.

Your goal is to always aim at the best possible match between what you are proposing and the RIGHTS of the other person. If, after a period of time, you find the gap between his RIGHTS and what you are offering cannot be fully closed, then perhaps it is time to revert to your backup plan (BATNA), which may be to say "thank you" and part on friendly terms, leaving open the potential to do business in the future.

Identify Current Choice

You have created a space of trust and safety for the other person. You have taken time to understand, thus respect, his model of the world. By asking questions, you've gained an understanding of what is important for him (RIGHTS). You also know what his current choice is, which could be as simple as doing nothing. You believe what you have to offer will meet his RIGHTS better than his current choice. Now, you must help him to consider this as a possibility.

Doubt or Question Current Choice

Your objective is to help the other person see how well his current choice satisfies his RIGHTS and potentially raises doubts or questions as to whether this is his best choice. There are a number of tools you can use, some of which you are already familiar with:

- Perceptual positions.
- Cartesian quadrants.
- Visualization and related methods to feel more resourceful.
- Precision model questions.
- Reframing.

  Changing the frame of an experience can have a major influence on how the other person perceives, interprets and reacts to a given experience. The purpose of reframing is to help him cast doubt on and expand beyond his current thoughts, beliefs, limitations and actions to become more resourceful and have more choice in finding solutions to his problems.

Explore Alternatives

The other person is doubting his current choice and is starting to explore the possibility that there may be a better course of action available. At this stage, you want to present one or more win-win alternatives that more fully meet his needs and that avoid or address some of the negative consequences of his current choice. If possible, involve the other person in developing alternatives that support mutual gain.

The tools used to raise doubts (e.g. perceptual positions) can be used at this stage to explore the potential of possible alternative choices.

Another useful approach is to explore the purpose behind his current choice. Far too often, influence opportunities go off the rails because one or both parties insist on finding a solution in the details before having reached an agreement on the overall intention. Indeed, it is not uncommon for one party to guess what the other person wants, and often this guess is off the mark. The key to moving past this is to explore the purpose behind the other person's current choice (in NLP terms—*chunk up*, move to more abstract levels of thought) until you and the other person agree. Once you agree, your task is to be more specific so that it is clear what needs to be done (in NLP terms—*chunk down*). However, you gain more specificity only as fast as you both maintain agreement. To chunk up on an idea, you can explore answers to the question, "What is the intention or purpose?" Although using different words, we were exploring this very question in the "So What?" exercise (section 3.5) as well as when we explored, "This is a solution to what problem?" in section 6.2. Once you reach a higher intention on which you both agree, you can begin to chunk down or look for different ideas or courses of action that support this intention by exploring questions such as:

- What is an example, component or part of this? If the higher intention is to create a healthy workplace where all staff can express their ideas, then an answer to this question may be, "Weekly staff meeting will include an agenda item on this topic chaired by someone other than management."
- What/who/where/when specifically? If the higher intention is for a couple with children to reignite the spark, then an answer to this question may be, "Each Friday hire a babysitter, so they can have dinner and a night out."

Address Objections and Misunderstandings
People will have objections, so expect them and handle them in a way that is respectful. The trust that you have worked hard to establish can be easily lost by inappropriately responding to objections. Avoid arguing with the other person. Respect his opinion and explore ways that both of you can work to address the issue.

Possible courses of action are:

- Determine the real objection. Sometimes the other person will present an objection that is not the real reason for rejecting your suggestion.
- Acknowledge that he has a valid point. By acknowledging his objection, you not only accept the point he has raised, you increase the rapport you have with him.
- Reframe a potential objection.
- Preframe potential issues: A preframe can be viewed as a reframe before the issue has been raised and is used to:
  o anticipate and address an objection or result that may disrupt a meeting at an inopportune time.
  o establish a focus or set boundaries.

In a sales context, you can anticipate and preframe potential major objections from your client or key points your competition may raise and handle them well before you present your offering and hence avoid being derailed at an inappropriate time.

Confirm New Choice

Rapport is being maintained, alternatives have been explored, objections have been addressed, his RIGHTS will be satisfied by this choice and for some reason the other person is not ready to commit. What can you do?

- Respect how he likes to buy. Many salespeople end up (unconsciously) selling themselves a product rather than the customer. They make the mistake of presupposing that the customer thinks the same way as they do.
- Give an extra nudge. Sometimes when we are close to an agreement, the other person needs a friendly supportive nudge. This can be done using language patterns such as a double bind, embedded command, tag question or using a metaphor. In each case, these are delivered with rapport and respect with the other person's well-being in mind.
- Make sure there are no misunderstandings.

Confirm your agreement in writing, if appropriate, and then take action.

7.2. IT'S A FOUR STEP PROCESS

At this stage, you know the RIGHTS your product satisfies and have a good idea of the other person's RIGHTS. Yet, there is a gap between what you are offering and his current choice[8]. If there is no gap, then, if you haven't done so, there is an agreement that needs to be recognized and put into action. This latter point is rather interesting. I'm sure you have experienced salespeople who have the sale in hand, yet do not recognize it. Why? Because either they do not have a good idea of your RIGHTS and the RIGHTS their product satisfies, or they are simply not paying attention and are fully wrapped up in their own sales process.

The gap that remains may be small or large and may be closed almost instantaneously. Or the process of closing the gap may play out over several months. It's all about changing beliefs.

Changing Beliefs

In an influence situation, the position you hold and the different position the other person holds are based on what each of you believe. These beliefs may be

---

8 No choice is also a choice. That is, if he is uncertain as to what to do, that is his current choice.

major significant beliefs or lightly held beliefs. To reach an agreement, one or both of you need to change your belief in order to reach a win-win agreement. For example:

- You are a manager: You believe a member of your staff needs to improve his performance. On the other hand, he believes he is performing well.
- You are a parent: You believe your son should be home by 10:00pm, he believes midnight is OK.
- You are a salesperson. You believe your product/service will meet your customer's needs. He believes your product/service is too expensive or will not perform to his expectation.

The belief change cycle is a naturally occurring process that each of us goes through when we move from one belief to another. A belief change that many of us have experienced illustrates this process:

- It begins with a **current choice**—a belief you hold. At one time, you may have believed in Santa Claus—a very powerful belief that had a major impact on your behaviors.
- New information leads you to **doubt or question** this belief. As you grow older, you gather information from your friends, parents, TV and other media, and gradually you begin to question your belief about Santa Claus.
- You reach a point where you begin to **explore alternatives** and are open to change—believing something else. Continuing to believe in Santa Claus in the face of new information or the teasing of friends leads you to consider alternatives.
- You **confirm a new choice**—a new belief, one that is either supported by this new information or maintains existing benefits or provides other perceived benefits, takes root. You now have a new belief and supporting strategies about Santa Claus that allows you to maintain the positive benefits (gifts) while avoiding the negative ones.

To change a belief, you pass through each of the above phases, even if the time in a specific phase is miniscule. Think about a belief that you have recently changed—e.g. change of opinion about a coworker, family member, choice of foods, choice of lifestyle. Did it not pass through these phases?

I remember when, some years ago, I was a strong supporter of a certain political party. Yes, they botched things here and there, but because I believed they were the best, I tended to ignore this evidence and focused on what supported my belief. Then a day came where I still supported this political party and I began to doubt some of their actions or policies. Eventually, I gathered enough information that I realized this political party was not right for my interests and I explored alternatives. Now I support a different political party. This process, if I remember correctly, took about half a year.

Belief change (or the influence process) can take about six months or more as illustrated in the above example or happen almost instantly—"I don't believe I will like your new recipe. Wow, this is good!"

Sometimes the belief that stops your client from accepting a proposed agreement is not about your idea, product or service; it is about you. He simply does not believe in you for some reason. I have often heard managers and staff complain that their senior management people do not buy into their ideas or suggested course of action unless it is presented or supported by an outside expert. They simply do not believe that their managers have the knowledge or ability to make this recommendation. This is fairly common as we all tend to pigeon-hole people. When they make suggestions/recommendations outside of the box we have put them in, we tend not to believe in them. As with any belief, this can be changed and it may take a while.

The four steps to bridging the gap are:

- Identify current choice and the degree to which it does or does not satisfy the other person's RIGHTS.
- Doubt or question current choice.
- Explore alternatives.
- Confirm new choice.

For ease of discussion, these four are presented as discrete sequential steps. However, in practice, more than one can occur at the same time and you may have to double back and repeat a certain step. For example, to increase your understanding of the other person's RIGHTS, you have asked questions to get clarity for yourself. In hearing and answering these questions, the other person also gained clarity in his RIGHTS, which may have raised doubts in his mind and already put him on a path of exploring what other choices are possible. Or prior to confirming a new choice, you may have to reinforce or add to the doubts he has about his current position.

7.3. IDENTIFY CURRENT CHOICE

You have created a space of trust and safety for the other person. You have taken time to respect his model of the world and, by asking questions, you've formed an understanding of what is important for him (RIGHTS) and his current choice. You believe what you have to offer will meet his RIGHTS better than his current choice.

During this and subsequent steps, employ active listening with appropriate questions to gain useful information. Also confirm or acknowledge what you have heard without agreeing or disagreeing by using neutral, empathetic and non-defensive words. For example, "I understand (appreciate) your concern about ...." And if you have made progress, summarize this, emphasizing those RIGHTS that you both share.

Example: Performance Appraisal

You are a manager conducting a performance appraisal with a staff member. You have asked him questions on what is important to him about his job and the choices he makes in carrying out his duties (RIGHTS).

This example is continued to illustrate possible actions in the following sections. If you are not a manager, think about your role as a parent or son/daughter supporting an elderly parent, or salesperson supporting a customer. This example is applicable to many different situations.

7.4. DOUBT OR QUESTION CURRENT CHOICE

You can tell people they have made the wrong choice. How useful is that? How do you feel if someone tells you that you have made the wrong choice or simply presents information to dispute your choices? It's far better to ask questions—questions that assist the other person to look at his choice from different perspectives and in so doing begin to wonder if he has made the best choice given his expressed needs.

Indeed, as you ask him questions to determine his RIGHTS, he may have already begun to doubt his current preferences and even started looking for alternative choices.

To raise doubts or question a current choice, there are a number of tools you can use, some of which you are already familiar with:

• Perceptual positions

   For a given situation (e.g. how a coworker interacts with a fellow worker), you can ask him to experience his actions from another person's point of view and suggest that he explore what it's like for the other person to be in a conversation with him. You can ask him what an independent third party (third position) would think about his actions and what suggestions this person would give him. Or ask him what could be the impact of his current choice on his workplace today and two years from now.

- Cartesian quadrants

  With regard to his choices, you can encourage him to explore the following
  questions from his perspective:

  - What will happen if I continue with my current choice?
  - What will happen if I change my current choice?
  - What will not happen if I continue with my current choice?
  - What will not happen if I change my current choice?

- Visualization and related methods to feel more resourceful.

  Sometimes we do not challenge our current choice because we do not feel
  resourceful. Here you can assist him in feeling more resourceful by using the
  ideas in section 4.7—particularly visualization and the exercise developed
  by Richard Bandler.

- Precision model questions.

  The precision model questions can help you and the other person gain more
  clarity on his choices and, as a result, may lead him to start questioning
  his choices.

Example: Performance Appraisal (continued)

Your staff member may have expressed his RIGHTS or choices solely from
his perspective without regard for his work team or employer. Using the
jargon of the precision model (you can translate this to appropriate words for
your situation), you may ask, "How, specifically, by making these choices,
are you addressing your RIGHTS, supporting your work team and contributing to this organization?"

Depending on what he has said about carrying out his duties, you may ask
other precision model questions such as:

- Who or what stops you from satisfying your RIGHTS and supporting
  your work team or contributing to this organization?
- How, specifically, can you improve to meet your RIGHTS and those
  of the company?
- How, specifically, do you see your approach as being better than our
  standard approach?

Help the Other Person Go Beyond Self-Imposed Limits

A picture frame places borders or boundaries around what can be seen in a
picture. In a similar fashion, the frames of reference the other person chooses

because of his beliefs about himself and others, his perceived role in life, and his perceived limitations in skills or abilities can limit what he believes. People are continually setting time frames, psychological boundaries and physical limits on what can or can't be done—often without any real thought about the consequences or the reality of those limitations.

Changing the frame of an experience can have a major influence on how your colleague perceives, interprets and reacts to a given experience. Knowing he has one hour to complete a task will most likely result in a different emotional state, approach and quality of work than if he knows he has one week to accomplish the same task. This illustrates how a change in frame—in this case a time frame—can have a significant impact on the choices the other person makes. In NLP, changing the frame of reference is called *reframing*. The purpose of reframing is to help the other person cast doubt on and expand beyond his current thoughts, beliefs, limitations and actions to become more resourceful and have more choice in finding solutions to his problems.

Perceptual positions, Cartesian quadrants and precision model questioning are forms of reframing as they help the other person step outside of his self-imposed limits.

Reframing goes on all around you
During the course of a typical day, you are often on the receiving end or provide different interpretations of a topic or action—to make someone feel better about themselves, to diminish someone else's accomplishments, to diminish or enhance your accomplishments (completed a resume recently?). An excuse is a reframe that attributes a different meaning or context to your behaviors. Politicians are masters at reframing. It seems no matter what happens, they can create a positive spin for themselves or a negative spin for their opponents.

Pay attention and notice when you or someone else is reframing an idea, action, situation, etc. Notice how the reframe changes your interpretation. Get good at reframing. It is a valuable tool, if used to help yourself or the other person.

Recently, I was at a resort in the Caribbean. The weather had been beautiful all week, except for a small amount of rain the past two mornings. I was at a trolley stop and overhead a group planning their next couple of days. One person suggested doing something the next morning, when a man piped up, "No, we need to avoid the morning as it rains every morning." (notice how he generalized his experience and limited his possibilities). Then another person who was not part of his party said, "Most mornings are lovely, it has only been the last two mornings." Thus, the person's interpretation was changed (reframed). I also suggest to you that, in the blink of an eye, it changed his belief (rains every morning) to being open to doubt, to open to believing something new, to accepting the new belief (it doesn't rain every morning). How often have you, with the skimpiest of information—rained the last two days—made a decision about yourself, someone else or a situation that was not true and that limited what was/is possible for you or others?

Change the meaning or the context

In NLP, there are two basic forms of reframes—*content* (or meaning) and *context* reframes. When helping someone see an issue from a different perspective, it is useful to ask yourself, "Is there a different meaning that I can raise that would allow him to see this situation differently or is there a context where this ability or action would be seen to be very valuable?" In the example above, it was about changing the meaning or interpretation that was assigned to each (and every) morning.

Content reframe

What you choose to focus on or how you interpret an event determines the content or meaning you have chosen to assign to it.

A content reframe is useful for statements such as, "I get annoyed when my boss stands behind me while I am working." Notice how this situation is given a narrow, specific meaning thus, limiting the speaker's resourcefulness and possible courses of action. To reframe this situation, remember the NLP presupposition, "every behavior has a positive intention" and explore:

- What other meaning could his boss' behavior have? This may lead you to asking the speaker "Is it possible he wants to help and doesn't know how to offer his assistance in any other way?"
- What is the positive value in the speaker's thoughts (behavior)? A possible reframe might be, "Isn't it great that you know your boundaries and you're not prepared to allow someone to violate them?"

Examples of content reframes:

During the 1984 U.S. presidential campaign, there was considerable concern about Ronald Reagan's age. Speaking during the presidential debate with Walter Mondale, Reagan said, "I will not make age an issue of this campaign. I am not going to exploit, for political purposes, my opponent's youth and inexperience." Reagan's age was not an issue for the remainder of the campaign!

When I was a senior manager for the Canadian government, my division was working on a major project. We were on a tight schedule and at a point where quality assurance was a critical function. The person handling this responsibility was a very capable woman who was a subcontractor from a consulting firm. Often subcontractors have the choice of being paid at the end of every month or receiving a larger percentage of their per diem by getting paid only when the consulting company is paid. In a government organization, the administrative and financial wheels can move very slowly. As a result, this woman had not been paid for some time. I pursued the issue as far as I could in my organization, but she still had not been paid. Finally, she came into my office very frustrated and angry, and told me that she would not be coming back to work until she was paid. I had done all I could to ensure she was paid and, being very clear on my outcome—delivery of this project on time and budget, I said to her in a calm voice, "Don't come back." Her head jerked up and she immediately saw the issue from a different perspective—late monthly payment versus no monthly paychecks. At which point, we sat down, had a friendly and productive conversation and she returned to work the next day, realizing that she needed to work things out with the consulting company. My reframe—don't come back—may be perceived as a little harsh, but I do believe it resulted in a win for both of us.

You are having a garage sale and you hope to sell an old dirty vase for twenty-five cents. That is, until you overhear someone say that it could be a valuable antique. In a flash, the meaning you have assigned has changed. In a similar way, some of us have a tendency to diminish or devalue our own worth and, perhaps, in the eyes of others we are worth a great deal more. For example, in a negotiation do you undervalue the contribution that you or your offering make, and thus give away what you have to offer for a lot less than it's worth?

A potentially valuable and simple reframe would be to ask the other person, "Is it possible another approach will meet your needs better than what you are doing now?" If he replies "yes," then you have established some doubt in his mind. In a similar way, you may ask, "Does your approach satisfy all of your needs?"

Context reframe

Almost all attributes or behaviors are useful or appropriate in some context. A context reframe is useful for statements such as, "I'm too young," or "I wish I didn't always focus on what might go wrong." In these situations, the other person has assumed that being young or exhibiting this behavior has little or no value. Your role is to discover when it can be of value by asking yourself the questions, "When would this attribute be viewed as a resource?" Or "Where would this behavior be viewed as useful? A possible reframe for the former might be, "Think of the advantage you have over the others because you're younger—you have time to learn new skills and to be more successful than they are." And for the latter, "Isn't noticing what might go wrong a great skill to have when you need to avoid potential problems?"

The first reframe changes the context of time, while the second changes the context to one of "avoiding potential problems."

Examples of context reframes:

A woman says, "I'm too giving of a person." She feels discouraged about how empathetic and caring she is toward others without any seeming return or acknowledgement. After some thought, you may say, "Is that not one of the most important abilities for a mother to have?"

When working for a corporation associated with the Canadian government, I was appointed the acting senior manager for their technology division to replace the previous manager who had suddenly left. The only technical background that I had was a course in a programming language that was on its way out. My appointment was temporary until they found a suitable replacement. The vacancy was advertised all across Canada and applications were due in about three months from when I assumed this role. By that time, I had cut the division's budget by about 20 percent and had significantly improved staff morale, to such a degree that they sent a delegation to the president asking that I continue in the job on a permanent basis. As well, I was really enjoying what I was doing. Therefore, I applied for the position going up against competition that had at least ten years of relevant experience and training and who had been on a career path for this very job. The interview board was composed of a senior manager from my organization and two highly respected technology experts whom I had never met before. I began the interview by establishing rapport. Even though two of the interviewers had technology backgrounds that far surpassed anything that I could even think of, the interview turned into a very animated and warm conversation. Going into the interview, I realized that I could not compete on my technology skills or experience. I needed to change the playing field to one where I was perceived to be at least competitive if not superior. As the job interview ended, I was asked if there was anything that I wanted to add. I concluded the interview by asking them the following question, "When you staff a position, would you rather hire the person who has all of the skills and little passion for the position or the person who can learn the skills and has a passion for making things happen?" In doing so, I moved the conversation from assessing candidates on skills alone to including a passion and relating this to what I had already accomplished. By the way, I got the job.

Additional points to consider

When presenting a reframe to another person:

- If you present the reframe in the form of a question or a metaphor, it will most likely be considered more fully than if you present it as a statement of fact.
- Make sure you have rapport and the person is open to hearing something different. I often begin with, "May I ask you a question?"
- You may believe your reframe is the best ever and yet it may not work for the other person—simply because he has a different model of the world than you do. Remember the NLP presupposition that there is no failure, only feedback, and explore other possible reframes.
- Avoid getting caught up in your own limitations. To offer an effective reframe, you must step outside of the other person's model of the world, which may be constrained by many of the same limiting beliefs/thoughts that you have.
- I do not make a big deal out of whether or not a reframe is a context or content reframe. Rather, I use these two ideas to help me develop a reframe that may make the difference.

7.5. EXPLORE ALTERNATIVES

The other person is beginning to doubt his current choice and is starting to explore the possibility that there may be a better course of action available. At this stage, you want to present one or more win-win alternatives that better meet his needs and avoid some of the negative consequences of his current choice. If possible, involve the other person in developing alternatives that support mutual gain.

Some of the tools you have been using so far can also be used here, for example:

- Perceptual positions

  You can ask him, "If you were me, your coworker, an independent observer, what alternatives would you suggest?" "If you were to look at this from our family or work environment perspective, what alternatives would have the most positive impact on the functioning of our family (work environment) in one year or five years from now?"

- Methods to feel more resourceful, e.g. visualization.

  It is much easier to step out of your narrow view and consider other alternatives when in a resourceful state.

- Precision model questions

  The precision model questions may have led him to doubt his current choice and in doing so lead him to explore what else is possible.

- Reframing

  Helping him see his choices and other choices with a different meaning or in a different context may have opened doors to a better choice.

Explore a Higher Intention

If you have taken time to explore the other person's RIGHTS, you have a good idea of how well your proposal satisfies his RIGHTS. If there is not complete agreement, you may want to explore a higher purpose on which you both agree. Without knowing his higher intention, both of you will most likely argue about the details and not reach a meaningful or win-win agreement.

Far too often, influence opportunities go off the rails because one or both parties insist on finding a solution in the details before having reached an agreement on the overall intention. Indeed, it is not uncommon for one party to guess what the other person wants, and often this guess is off the mark. The key to moving past this is to explore the purpose behind the other person's choice; that is, chunk up until you and the other person agree and then to chunk back down to the details only as fast as you both maintain agreement. To chunk up on an idea, you can explore answers to the question, "What is the intention or purpose?" Although using different words, we were exploring this very question in the "So What?" exercise (section 3.5) as well as when we explored "This is a solution to what problem?" and "Sometimes clients have the solution" in section 6.2.

Once you reach a higher intention on which you both agree, you can begin to chunk down or look for different ideas or courses of action that support this intention by exploring questions such as:

- What is an example of this? If the higher intention is for your child to show respect to his teacher, then an answer to this question may be, "Say good morning to your teacher when she enters the classroom."
- What is a component or part of this? If the higher intention is to purchase a vacation that the whole family can enjoy, then an answer to this question may be "A place that has water sports."
- What/who/where/when specifically? If the higher intention is for better customer service, then an answer to this question may be, "Training for frontline staff by the end of the month."

Being able to chunk up (more general or abstract) or down (more specific or detailed) on an idea can pay major dividends at this stage of the influence process.

Examples:

During one NLP practitioner training session, we were reviewing material from previous days and considering how the students could use it. One woman from out of town described how she had called her husband and asked him what he wanted to do upon her return. He immediately suggested, "Let's go to the cottage for the weekend." Having been away from home for over a week, she did not relish the idea of repacking immediately and going to the cottage. Recalling the chunking process, she asked him in a supportive tone, "You would like to go to the cottage—for what purpose?" His answer was, "To spend time with you." This approach opened up many more options for her to pursue that would meet her husband's need and that would also be acceptable to her. While I don't remember what they decided to do, I do recall that she was very pleased and said it avoided a possible troublesome argument.

Thinking laterally, which is simply the process discussed above—first chunk up, then chunk down—helps uncover other possible courses of action. Suppose you want to take your child to an event and your car is not available. To identify alternatives, first chunk up. For instance, what is the purpose of your car? One possible chunk up is to transport people. Next, by chunking down from the context of "transport people," you can easily identify many different ways to get from one place to another rather than using your car (some of which may be a lot more fun)—for example, bicycle, bus, train, airplane, horse or walking. That is, you can easily think beyond the norm and potentially come up with an innovative solution that meets both your needs.

Example: Performance Appraisal (continued)

You have maintained rapport with your staff member, you have a good understanding of his RIGHTS and the choices he has been making. Through asking precision model questions, he is questioning his choices and is open to exploring alternative ways of supporting his team and the organization.

At this time, you decide to explore the intention behind his RIGHTS and past choices. You continue to explore this higher intention until you reach a point where you both agree. E.g. healthy functioning of the workplace where people respect each other and work to earn the respect of others. Sounds good. Now you have to translate this into concrete actions by him and you. Together you explore what these actions might be. That is, become more detailed while maintaining agreement on the overall purpose and subsequent steps.

Address Objections and Misunderstandings

People will have objections, so expect them and handle them in a way that is respectful. The trust that you have worked hard to establish can be easily lost by inappropriately responding to objections. Avoid arguing with him. Respect his opinion and explore ways that both of you can work to address the issue.

Why do people have objections?

- He is still holding onto original choice. There is something important in his choice that you have failed to uncover and address. Perhaps you need to explore the RIGHTS his choice satisfies.
- He has doubts about your suggested alternative. From his perspective, you have not presented your alternative suggestion in a way that addresses his needs. He perceives a negative that you have not addressed or he perceives you as too rigid when it comes to holding onto your point of view. Far too often, people focus on the obvious features of their offering rather than satisfying the other person's RIGHTS. Have you missed identifying or addressing something that is important to him? Get curious. Ask questions or think about modifying your suggested alternative.
- He has doubts about you. You may remind him of someone he does not trust or, in a previous interaction with you, he may feel that the final agreement did not satisfy his RIGHTS.

Determine the real objection

Sometimes the other person will present an objection that is not the real reason for rejecting your suggestion. To find out the real underlying objection, ask him if you were to satisfy his stated objection, would he buy your product/service. If he then says no, inquire if there is another objection and repeat the process. You may have to do this several times to find the real objection.

Take time to determine his outcome and RIGHTS that are not being met and hence the root of his objection. Perhaps you can satisfy these in some other way or by making minor adjustments to your offering.

In some cases, it is not an objection; he simply has a buying strategy that includes a period of time. That is, he needs some time—one hour or several weeks—to assess your proposal before making a decision.

Acknowledge he has a valid point

People like to feel they have valid points. By acknowledging his objection, you not only accept the point he raised—you increase the rapport you have with him. You can reply to him by saying, "I appreciate or understand why you would feel that way, and have you considered … ?" Or you may seek to clarify his objection by summarizing it using his words (these words are the ones that are most important to him). By restating his objection, it will be clear to both of you what needs to be addressed. If there is some part of his objection that you do not fully understand, use the precision model to gain increased clarity. Restating an objection will direct the conversation in an amicable manner and lessen the opportunity for dispute. In this way, you show that you are listening and you demonstrate a desire to resolve the situation.

Reframe a potential objection

Recall that Ronald Reagan addressed a potential major objection to his candidacy during the 1984 U.S. presidential campaign by giving a different interpretation that took the objection right off the table: "I will not make age an issue of this campaign. I am not going to exploit, for political purposes, my opponent's youth and inexperience."

To reframe an objection, explore the positive intention behind it. Your boss says to you, "I don't like the idea of receiving your report first thing Monday morning; I want to have it by end of day on Friday." You explore his objection by asking questions and find out that he does not want you working on the weekend and that you should be spending that time with your family. With this new information, you tell him that to have the report done for Friday will mean working Thursday evening when you have a family function planned and your Saturday afternoon is wide open.

Being able to acknowledge and reframe objections is an important skill.

Preframe potential issues
A reframe provides an opportunity to explore different interpretations of an idea, product, service or activity. A reframe is used after an interpretation or issue that in some way limits what is possible has been raised.

A preframe can be viewed as a reframe before an issue is raised and is used to:

- Anticipate and address an objection or result that may disrupt a meeting at an inopportune time.
- Establish a focus or set boundaries.

I am an NLP trainer and an essential part of an NLP training is for students to experience a significant change/shift in how they see themselves, others or the world around them. To accomplish this they must step out of the world of "what you know you know" into the world of "what you don't know you don't know." Often when people fully and truly step into the world of "what you don't know you don't know," they experience confusion or their mind may go blank. If they are not prepared for this, they may not feel safe or lose faith in the process and not wish to proceed further. I preframe this possible experience by saying something like, "At some point, you may experience confusion or your mind may go blank and I think this is great, because it indicates you have stepped out of your current world that is holding you back and are now in a new place that opens up the possibility of exploring new ideas and ways of being." Given that the students have accepted my preframe, then later during the class, they are OK if they experience confusion or their mind goes blank and are more likely to fully explore what is possible for them.

In a sales context, you can anticipate and preframe potential major objections from your client or key points your competition may raise and handle them well before you present your offering and hence avoid being derailed at an inappropriate time.

Preframing can be used to inform others as to how they may choose to perceive a product, service, idea or person. For example, if I introduce a speaker by saying, "It's not often that you get to meet a person who has had such a positive influence on creating healthy work environments," then I have directed your expectations in a certain direction.

A good agenda or description preframes a meeting or presentation in terms of what will and will not be covered thus creating a focus and minimizing complaints that someone's favorite topic was not discussed. You can also preframe many influence situations as a shared search for win-win solutions.

Be aware that your behaviors (past and current), as perceived and interpreted by others, preframe current and subsequent conversations/interactions. That is, based on how you have interacted with others or what you have accomplished to date, people will make a decision about how trustworthy you are, to what degree your ideas will be considered and whether or not you have the expertise/ability to deliver what you promise. Here, behaviors are interpreted in a wide context, for example, the words you use, your tone of voice, your body language, the way you dress and who you choose as friends.

7.6. CONFIRM NEW CHOICE

Even though you both may agree on the higher intention, you may not be able to satisfy all of his RIGHTS with your proposed alternative or other alternatives that have been raised. If both of you cannot find room to compromise, you have the option of going to your BATNA (Best Alternative to a Negotiated Agreement), which may mean walking away while maintaining rapport so that you can enter into other discussions at a future date.

On the other hand, rapport is being maintained, alternatives have been explored, objections have been addressed, his RIGHTS will be satisfied by this agreement and for some reason he is not ready to commit. What can you do?

Respect How He Likes to Buy and Use It

Many salespeople end up (unconsciously) selling themselves a product rather than the customer. They make the mistake of presupposing that the customer thinks the same way as they do.

Each of us has a preferred way (habit, ritual) to buy an idea, product or service, and context may have an influence. You may view the way that another person prefers to buy as strange, annoying, or "you've got to be kidding!" However, to him in some way it feels comfortable, familiar and safe. Often this habit or strategy for making a decision or buying something is so ingrained in him, operating at an unconscious level, that it is simply a way of life. "Doesn't everyone do it that way?" You have the same thoughts about how you prefer to buy. Therefore, when you approach someone to influence him to buy your idea, product or service, you just assume he will buy it exactly the same way you do. If you prefer lots of information, then this is what you will provide to the other person. If he likes to see things and you don't, you will tend to avoid this. Unfortunately, this can create a disconnect, have a negative impact on rapport and possibly scuttle any agreement.

Be flexible and present your idea, product or service in the way that the other person prefers.

> To effectively communicate, we must realize that we are all different in the way we perceive the world and use this understanding as a guide to our communication with others.
>
> —*Anthony Robbins*

I suggest that, if you have known and interacted with someone for some time, then, without asking him, you already have a good idea of how he likes to buy. If you are not aware of his buying strategy, you can ask questions, as outlined in section 6.2 "Ask questions." That is, inquire if he has purchased something similar and ask him to describe this process.

As you have been asking questions and paying attention, have you noticed that the other person has a preference for one or more of visual, auditory, kinesthetic or digital? Have you been paying attention to the meta programs he uses? You have a good match between his RIGHTS and what your product delivers. Now is the time to get an agreement. For example:

- If he is visual, help him see the similarities in your product and his RIGHTS.
- If he is kinesthetic, help him get a feeling for how they dovetail together.
- If he has a tendency for Away From, help him recognize what he will avoid or get rid of (using his words).
- If he is Externally referenced, point out what the experts say or how his friends will react.
- An Options person will tend to avoid committing until you point out that by committing now will keep his options open.
- For a procedures person, explain that there are five key steps to reaching a win-win agreement. List these steps, then point out, one at a time, that he has now completed steps 1, 2 and 3 in that order. A procedures person loves procedures and, once he starts a procedure, he feels compelled to complete it.
- For a person who needs a Period of Time before committing, respect this and ask if you can contact him at the end of that time period and if, in the interim, he decides to purchase your product or needs more information, to please contact you.

Some key aspects of my buying strategy are:

- Some visual, very little auditory (if a salesman tries to follow me around the store and talk to me, I have a real urge to leave), not a great deal of kinesthetic (although everyone's buying strategy has a feeling at the end about the decision they made) and lots of facts and figures (digital)—initial cost, cost to maintain, gas mileage, pages per minute, processing speed.
- Slight preference for Toward compared to Away From. I do focus on achieving, attaining while paying attention to what needs to be fixed.
- Mostly Internal with some External. When I published my first book *Live Your Dreams Let Reality Catch Up*, I knew what I wanted to say. So other than having an editor polish the English, nobody saw or commented on the content until after it was published—now that's an Internal focus.
- Options rather than Procedures. I like to have choice and consider at least three different options. If I am buying a laser printer, I need to assess at least three different laser printers. When I was a senior manager (before I knew NLP), I am sure that I frustrated my staff on more than one occasion. If staff brought me one suggested approach to solve an issue, I would "tear it apart" in order to construct at least two other options to consider. As a consultant, I remember submitting proposals with at least three possible courses of action—even if the client did not request it, because that's how I like to buy.

- Fairly balanced between Sameness and Difference.
- Tend to be Reactive. In addition I prefer to digest the information for a period of time, which can be as long as two or three weeks. As a result, I am not prone to impulse buying and will walk away from a sale if I have not had sufficient time to consider my purchase. A good sale will leave me conflicted as I like to save money and also want time to fully consider my purchase.

Remember to use my own words for greater impact. I might say to you, "I need to eat healthy." Although, "Our foods will help you to avoid being sick," may mean the same to you, it will mean something quite different to me. One statement is Toward and the other Away From, and the word "healthy," which may be very important to me, is missing in your response.

You may find how I buy different or strange. However, it works for me. If you want to sell me something, the more you can accommodate my buying strategy, the more comfortable (in rapport) I will be with you and the more inclined I will be to buy your idea, product or service.

People have distinctly different buying strategies. For example, some may purchase by simply looking for something that meets their RIGHTS and buy it. For a person who makes effective quick decisions, a salesperson who goes through a slow cautious sales pitch is just an annoyance. Similarly, for those long written e-mail or webpage sales pitches that repeat themselves several times and seem to go on forever. Obviously this approach does not work for me, but it does for others.

Give an Extra Nudge

Sometimes when we are close to an agreement, the other person needs a friendly supportive nudge.

Confirm they are making the right decision

The majority of people, when buying something, want you to not only tell them what to do but to reassure them they are making the right decision. This is where you can once more illustrate how their RIGHTS and the RIGHTS provided by your offering are a good match. And you can also use some of the following language patterns to gently encourage them.

Help them decide by using a double bind

A double bind suggests to the other person that there are only two possibilities and it is a matter of choosing one of them. In reality, the other person has lots of choice.

Examples (delivered with rapport and respect):

You may say to your child, "Do you want to go to bed now or immediately following your favorite TV show?" Here you are giving your child the illusion of choice. In either case, if he accepts the choice, he is going to bed at a time that is acceptable to you.

You may say to a coworker, "Will you have this done today or by lunch tomorrow?" Again the illusion of choice and either option results in your needs being met.

I have used double binds a number of times, with great results. In one situation, I was dealing with a large multi-national company and getting the runaround from their staff. Fortunately, I had documented all of our communications. Finally, I wrote a letter to each member of the company's board of directors, with an attachment providing full details concerning how I had been treated. The final sentence of my letter was the following: "Either you fully support how your staff has handled this or you commit to resolving it in a way that is mutually satisfactory to both parties." (Notice the double bind.) Two weeks later, I received an offer that exceeded my expectations!

Use embedded commands
This is a command that is included as part of a larger sentence. In writing, the embedded command is marked by the use of italics, and in speech, it is marked by a subtle change in voice tonality or body language that is picked up by the reader's or listener's unconscious. For the embedded command use a statement or command tonality or syntax, even if the sentence is a question.

Examples (delivered with rapport and respect):

"I will not suggest to you that *doing well in school will be easy.*"

"Do you think you should *tell your friends about this book.*" Notice, I have purposely omitted the question mark.

In order to make sense of these two sentences, what do you have to think about?

And please avoid saying something such as, "Don't *get angry* when I tell you this."

Use tag questions
A tag question is designed to soften resistance or ratify the agreement. A tag question follows a more direct, emphatic statement or question. It is used to ensure that the listener has consciously heard what you said and encourages him to actually manifest the implied action. It has the structure of a question and the tonality or syntax of a statement or command.

Examples (delivered with rapport and respect):

"Your perception of school is changing, *isn't it.*"

"You want to reach an agreement today, *don't you.*"

"You can easily use tag questions, *can't you!*"

Exercise:
Construct at least three sentences using each of the above language patterns. I know you will *create some great examples*, won't you. I'm not sure if you want to *do the exercise now* or in five minutes after you *read the descriptions one more time*.

Communicate through a story or figure of speech
A metaphor is an indirect way of communicating through a figure of speech or story. It can provide you with an effective way to communicate with another person at an unconscious level by offering solutions or suggestions (perhaps in the form of a fairy tale) or to quickly make a point. Recently, a friend and business colleague was modifying a highly successful course to satisfy a potential client. Essentially, he was diluting the content. I made my point to him very clearly by saying, "A fine wine is no longer a fine wine when diluted." Metaphors are part of everyone's life, from the bedtime story, through the parables in the Bible, to the way you think of yourself and the way you dress. If the other person speaks in metaphors, pay attention and then present your closing arguments in the same metaphor, it can have a powerful unconscious effect.

Metaphors can be used in situations where you would like your listener to detach from their current situation and consider other possibilities. This is especially so wherever there is potential for resistance, opposition or conflict. Metaphors provide you with helpful and useful communication and negotiation tools. It is difficult to argue with a good metaphor.

The quotes I have used in this book are metaphors that quickly and succinctly make or ratify my point. This is particularly true if you are Externally referenced or have a high regard for the person being quoted.

Next Steps

Make sure there is no misunderstanding
You have just reached a win-win agreement that you both fully support. But have you? Far too often, your understanding of what has been agreed to is not the same as what the other person expects. For example: you are a manger and have just agreed with a staff member that his report is fully acceptable. You have asked him to make copies and have it distributed to each member of the executive committee as soon as possible. Sounds good. Unfortunately, your interpretation of "as soon as possible" is by the end of the day and his is by the end of the week.

If the agreement or relationship (business or personal) is important, make sure you write it down with sufficient detail to avoid later disagreements. Many of the agreements that I have made in the past were based on a handshake. A handshake agreement is quick, convenient and, unfortunately, has gotten me into difficulty on many occasions. Speaking from experience, handshake agreements can put strains on valuable relationships. With a verbal agreement, there can be misunderstandings. In addition, if the agreement spans several months, it can morph into something different as each of you pursue what is most important. Since nothing is written down, the only thing you have to rely on is your respective memories, and they can change over time.

If appropriate, make sure your agreement addresses costs, action steps and accountabilities. Then deliver what you promised and often more.

Take action
Be proactive in holding up your end of the agreement. Without blowing your horn, be seen as fully supporting the agreement. Hold yourself and the other person accountable in delivering what has been promised. Follow-up with the other person to ensure you have fully met your part of the agreement. I can't tell you how many times I have made a major purchase and never heard from the salesperson again. Yet, in business, referrals can be the difference between just getting by and being successful.

Example: Performance Appraisal (continued)
> You present the win-win agreement, as you understand it, respecting your staff member's model of the world and how he likes to buy into an idea or proposed course of action, including using his choice of words. Making sure there is no disagreement and you both understand what is intended, you both sign a document that indicates your respective responsibilities with timeframes and consequences. Now take action.

> Take advantage of every opportunity to prac-
> tice your communication skills so that when
> important occasions arise, you will have
> the gift, the style, the sharpness, the clar-
> ity, and the emotions to affect other people.
> —*Jim Rohn*

Index

About the Author:
Roger Ellerton, PhD, CMC

ROGER IS PASSIONATE about helping others get what they desire in life. As a longtime successful businessman, university professor, NLP trainer/coach, public speaker, author and parent, he has first-hand experience with the personal/professional balancing act required in these busy times. He is a former tenured faculty member at the University of New Brunswick, an executive in the Canadian federal government, a certified management consultant (CMC) and he has been listed in the *International Who's Who in Education*.

Roger believes that each of us can achieve the success we desire by developing our authentic selves, mastering internal and external congruence and taking charge of our lives. He is a certified NLP trainer and has been delivering NLP, personal growth and business seminars and coaching services since 1996. Participants often remark how much fun it is being in his classes, how clearly he presents the material and how ready and willing he is to answer their questions and provide insights they have long been searching for.

For over twenty years, Roger has been a student of personal development methodologies. He continues to transform his own life while assisting others from all walks of life and all ages to learn, to address challenges at work and at home and to get more of what they desire in life. He is the father of four, an avid gardener and nature lover and he enjoys lending a hand to others.

He is the author of four books: *Live Your Dreams Let Reality Catch Up: NLP and Common Sense for Coaches, Managers and You*; *Live Your Dreams Let Reality Catch Up: 5 Step Action Plan*; *Parents' Handbook: NLP and Common Sense Guide for Family Well-Being* and *NLP Techniques Anyone Can Use* and of over sixty articles on NLP. Roger received his BSc. and MSc. from Carleton University in Ottawa, Canada, and his PhD from Virginia Tech, Blacksburg, Virginia, USA.

Roger is the founder and managing partner of Renewal Technologies Inc. For more information on his seminars, coaching and consulting services, visit www.renewal.ca.

16177015R00085

Made in the USA
San Bernardino, CA
21 October 2014